What people are saying about …

What's It Like to Be Married to Me?

"*What's It Like to Be Married to Me?* by Linda Dillow is a phenomenal book; in fact, it may well be the *best* book on marriage I have ever read. If you want to honor God in your marriage, if you want deeper intimacy with your spouse, if you want to become more like Christ, please, read this book. It is a rare and signature achievement that combines a penetrating look at marriage with practical spiritual formation. If all this sounds overstated, let me assure you that it is actually the opposite: Words fail me to describe just how marvelous this book really is."

Gary Thomas, writer in residence at Second Baptist Church in Houston and author of *Sacred Marriage*

"Every wife needs to read this book! Linda Dillow, as usual, is practical, insightful, and grounded. Not only will you understand yourself better with each page, but the journey will take you deep into the heart of the marriage you've always wanted. Don't miss out on this message."

Drs. Les and Leslie Parrott, founders of RealRelationships.com and authors of *Love Talk*

"From her vast biblical wisdom and experience, Linda has crafted a masterpiece that calls us to regard marriage as one of God's highest callings. Whatever the season of your marriage, you will be inspired, instructed, and encouraged by Linda's powerful and timely message."

Sally Clarkson, speaker, director of Mom Heart Ministry, and author of six books including *The Mission of Motherhood*

"Linda Dillow knows marriage. Through her extensive ministry to women, she has 'heard it all.' And through her years of study, she understands God's way. Most impressive, she has lived the message with her husband, Jody. Thanks, Linda, for this labor of love for all of us who want to see 'Well Done' on the marriage line of our final report card."

Roc Bottomly, pastor, senior fellow for Marriage Studies at Focus on the Family Institute, and author of *The Promised Power*

"As someone who travels, speaks, and writes with Linda Dillow, I've witnessed the gut-wrenching secret choices she's made in her own marriage as she's died to her own selfishness and lived to please God. This book and the stories within are so honest they will make your teeth hurt. Only read it if you're willing to be changed from the inside out."

Lorraine Pintus, speaker, writing coach, and author of *Jump Off the Hormone Swing*

"Is it okay to say there were times I wanted to throw this book across the room? Sometimes the truth hurts—but how vital that we hear it. Linda Dillow delicately weaves her words among the tough questions and the truths of Scripture. Putting these truths into practice will change your perspective, your marriage, and your life."

Kathy Cordell, life coach, speaker, and founding president of Women of Worship

"With tenderness, depth, humor, and spiritual understanding, Linda Dillow has carefully chosen topics that will impact any marriage. The book is brimming with practical ways to implement change. No one can read this book and remain the same."

Mimi Wilson, coauthor of *Once-A-Month Cooking, Holy Habits,* and *Trusting in the Goodness of God*

"Compelling, provocative, authentic, and practical! Linda invites the reader to focus the mirror on her own soul so that she might gain a transparent view of how she is perceived in her marriage. Whether you've been married five years or fifty, this book will challenge you to honestly consider the question *What's it like to be married to me?*"

Becky Harling, speaker and author of *Finding Calm in Life's Chaos, Rewriting Your Emotional Script,* and *Freedom From Performing*

"Linda's book is an absolute inspiration to stop the destructive pattern of blaming and criticizing our husbands and look at ourselves, challenging us to be honest about our attitudes and choices."

Cyndy Sherwood, author of *Road Map to Healing* and director of His Healing Light Ministries

"*What's It Like to Be Married to Me?* impacted me profoundly and brought my own marriage into focus more clearly as the joyous and holy calling it is, rather than as a duty or obligation. Rich with Scripture, poignant examples, and practical exercises, this book clearly identifies and forges a path to a more satisfying marriage by simply revealing the loving and healing choices a wife can make on behalf of the man she loves."

Shannon Wexelberg, worship leader, songwriter, and artist

"Whether you are contemplating marriage, are a newlywed, or have been married for decades, this book will have a profound impact on your heart. Be brave and ask these dangerous questions in your women's Bible studies or small groups, and watch God transform lives and marriages."

Judy Dunagan, director of women's ministries at Woodmen Valley Chapel in Colorado Springs, Colorado

"Please, please, please give this book to every young married woman you know! We have so few positive role models on what it means to be a godly wife, and this book gives us a roadmap on how to live by design not default. Linda has taught me how to define my goals as a wife, empowered me with practical steps to make those goals a reality, and encouraged me to humbly cry, 'Change me, Lord!'"

Eva Daniel, married seven months

"I have had the joy of leading a *What's It Like to Be Married to Me?* pilot study and saw the Holy One move in the lives of the women, including my own. Our hearts were softened and our actions began to change to deeply internal desires to please our Beloved by pleasing the beloved husband He gave us."

Bev DeSalvo, pastor's wife, Temple, Texas

"I have never been more challenged and encouraged as a wife as I was while reading this book. It is a dangerous book—one that will radically challenge your view of God's call on you life as a wife. It's one I will read again and again."

Dr. Juli Slattery, author and psychologist
with Focus on the Family

"If you desire to ponder and explore profound questions concerning your role as a wife, if you are willing to pray dangerous prayers, and if you want the best marriage possible, then this book is for you."

Cynthia Heald, speaker and author of the
best-selling Becoming a Woman of … series,
including *Becoming a Woman of Simplicity*

What's it like to be Married to Me?

And Other Dangerous Questions

LINDA DILLOW

David C Cook®
transforming lives together

To every wife who is brave enough to ask,

What's It Like to Be Married to Me?

WHAT'S IT LIKE TO BE MARRIED TO ME?
Published by David C Cook
4050 Lee Vance Drive
Colorado Springs, CO 80918 U.S.A.

David C Cook U.K., Kingsway Communications
Eastbourne, East Sussex BN23 6NT, England

The graphic circle C logo is a registered trademark of David C Cook.

Personal accounts throughout, including survey responses and written accounts, are used with permission, and some names have been changed for privacy purposes.

The Web site addresses recommended throughout this book are offered as a resource to you. These Web sites are not intended in any way to be or imply an endorsement on the part of David C Cook, nor do we vouch for their content.

LCCN 2010940550
ISBN 978-1-4347-0056-8
eISBN 978-0-7814-0609-3

© 2011 Linda Dillow

The Team: Terry Behimer, Liz Heaney, Amy Kiechlin, Caitlyn York, Karen Athen
Cover Design: JWH Graphic Arts, James Hall
Cover Image: Rights-managed, Getty Images, Sophie Broadbridge

Printed in the United States of America
First Edition 2011

8 9 10 11 12 13 14 15 16 17

Contents

Acknowledgments

I am thankful to God for:

My husband, Jody, who believes in me and pushes and encourages me to be all God wants me to be.

My coauthor and soul sister, Lorraine Pintus, who prayed for this book, read every word, and showed me how to make the words sing.

My editor, Liz Heaney, who worked so hard to make up for my "brain weakness." This book flows because Liz is the "Super Editor." She is also my friend.

The Cook Team: Dan Rich. I said I wouldn't follow you, but here I am. It is a joy to team with you! Terry Behimer: Your counsel moved this book to a new level. Your friendship made it fun! Amy Kiechlin, Caitlyn York, Karen Athen: Your work made this book better!

Every wife who gave permission to use her story in this book. All your names are changed, but I think you are brave, and your stories will pour hope and healing into every wife who reads these pages. God is grateful to you, and I am too.

To the special women in the pilot Bible study: Chee-Hwa Tan, Judy Dunagan, Valerie Cox, Darlene Kordic, Jodi Nunn, Penny Semmelbeck, Nanci McAlister, Deb Leach, Debbie Wood, Debbie Eng, Colleen Flora. You helped so much to shape this book and study!

To the special women who did the Bible study by email: Bev DeSalvo, Kathy Cordell, Sandi Funkhauser. Your comments were such a help!

By Design, Not Default

I played the roving reporter and asked women why they got married. Here are some of their answers:

The truth? Well, all my friends were getting married and the whole dream dress, dream day thing—I just wanted to be the Princess Bride too.

Obviously, it was because I was in love—I had found "the man of my dreams."

It was time—the clock was ticking, and it was time to move on to marriage and kids.

Kevin was my knight in shining armor who rescued me from a bipolar mom and alcoholic father.

I couldn't seem to make enough money to live the way I wanted to live. Trevor offered me security and the lifestyle I'd always wanted.

Women are a bit complicated. We want security, companionship, a lover, a soul mate, a fixer-of-things. Men are more simple. Consider the following newspaper ad:

> *Single black female seeks male companionship, ethnicity unimportant. I'm a very good-looking girl who LOVES to play. I love long walks in the woods, riding in your pickup truck, hunting, camping and fishing trips, cozy winter nights lying by the fire. Candlelight dinners will have me eating out of your hand. I'll be at the front door when you get home from work, wearing only what nature gave me.*
>
> *Call (404) 875–6420 and ask for Daisy. I'll be waiting.*[1]

Fifteen thousand men responded to this ad, wanting to talk with Daisy. Guess who answered the phone? The Atlanta Humane society. Daisy was an eight-week-old black Labrador retriever.

People marry for different reasons, but one man definitely takes the prize for the most unique reason. How I laughed when I read the following advertisement, which was said to appear in the want ads of a New York newspaper:

> *Farmer with 160 irrigated acres wants marriage-minded woman with tractor. When replying, please show picture of tractor.*[2]

I certainly didn't marry to gain a piece of farm equipment—or equipment of any kind! I married Jody because I wanted to be his lover and best friend, forever. One of the most beautiful verses of Scripture shows us the heart of a young bride as she describes her feelings for her husband. She has set forth the physical attributes of her beloved and ends with this statement:

"His mouth is full of sweetness
And he is wholly desirable.
This is my beloved and this is my friend." (Song 5:16)

A perfect combination: a lover and best friend, all wrapped up in one package called a husband. My neighbor Val showed me this note her husband had hidden under her pillow before he left on a business trip.

Dearest Val,

By now you are missing me. I want you to know that I love you and I am thinking of you even now. I miss every minute that I have to be away from you. I would much rather be holding you in my arms, pressing my lips against yours.

What I miss most of all is having a good walk and talking with you. I cherish having you to talk to and share with—someone who really wants to understand me and love me. I will be back soon. I love you a LOT.

Your lover,
Marc

This note graphically illustrates this perfect combo: a lover whose arms and lips you long for; a best friend whose deep communication and companionship you miss. This is what we dreamed of when we walked down the aisle and said, "I do."

I hope this is your everyday reality with your husband.

For many, though, the dream fades, and real life takes over. Children, jobs, house payments, and an economic downswing cause your lover/best-friend intimacy with your husband to slide down in your priorities. One day you wake up and say, "Where did the intimacy go? And how do I get it back?"

As I've spoken around the world, thousands of women have shared with me their questions, their hopes, and their dreams for their marriages. What I see happening in marriages today prompted me to write this book.

I'm angry.

I remember as a new bride in 1964 hearing Dr. Bill Bright, founder of Campus Crusade for Christ, quote a Harvard sociologist who said that one out of every two marriages ended in divorce. But in Christian marriages, it was very different. Only 1 out of every 1,015 marriages ended in divorce.[3] I felt proud. Being a Christian made a difference. That is no longer the case. Today, one out of every two marriages ends in divorce—and it is the same for those who know Christ and those who don't. What happened?

I'm sad.

Of the 50 percent of couples who stay married, many are angry and resentful. Others are simply resigned. They're living by default, not design. They're hanging on in marriage because it is the right thing to do. They stay because of the kids. They've given up and settled for ho hum, status quo. It shouldn't be this way.

I'm filled with hope.

I refuse to settle for mediocrity. I refuse to live out scripts handed to me by the media, by mothers, by anyone other than God. He is the Creator of marriage, and He has a design for you and for me. I'm filled with hope that you can be different, that your marriage can be different.

I wrote this book for all wives: those in good marriages and those in not-so-good. I wrote this book to encourage you as a wife, to help you change the things you can because I strongly believe that Christian marriages should—and can—be different. As part of my research, I surveyed five hundred Christian wives about the best and worst things they did in their marriages. I've seen the hurt in their eyes, and I've cried with them. I've prayed for them. I've asked God, "What will help Your precious women be all You desire them to be as wives?" I believe His answer to my question is this: *Ask them Dangerous Questions about themselves.* So, my friend, I will ask you the same Dangerous Questions I ask myself.

The title of this book, *What Is It Like to Be Married to Me?,* asks the overarching question. Too often we focus on all the things about our husbands that we don't like and wish we could change. You know what it is like to be married to your mate, but how often do you think about what it is like for him to be married to you? If you woke up tomorrow and discovered you were married to you, would you be delighted? Or would you be devastated? I believe that if you are willing to ask yourself this question and let me guide you to the Designer's personal answers for you and your marriage, you will find what Janee discovered doing the pilot Bible study: "This marriage study is life- and heart-changing."

To guide you in discovering what it is like to be married to you, this book will discuss seven Dangerous Questions:

1. What is really important to me?
2. What does it feel like to be my husband?
3. Am I willing to change my attitude?
4. What will it take for me to get close to you?
5. What is it like to make love to me?
6. Why do I want to stay mad at you?
7. Is it possible to grow together when things fall apart?

You'll see that each Dangerous Question contains several short insights meant to help you answer the Dangerous Question. You can read each Dangerous Question in one sitting, or you can read each one over a period of days or weeks. Do what works best for you.

I want this book to be practical, and so I've included exercises and ideas to help you put the concepts and insights into action. Don't read on until you have done these exercises. You'll need a separate journal or notebook. These exercises are really important. And to get the most for *you,* find a friend (or a group) and do the Bible study at the back of the book. (See page 209.) God's Word brings transformation.

It isn't fun to ask ourselves Dangerous Questions like these. It can be difficult and even threatening. But I believe that by honestly reflecting on these questions and by seeking God's help and wisdom, a wife can move to a place where she can say, "Being married to me is really pretty good." And maybe she'll even be able to affirm, "Being married to me is *better* than pretty good."

But even if we can say that, none of us is where we want to be.

When I was thirty-four, I wrote, "I want to work as hard at my marriage as if I were striving to be the president of a company." Thirty-four more years have passed since I made that statement. Looking back over these years, how did I do?

Did I work hard at creating a home that pleased him? Yes.

Did I seek to honor him before our children? I tried very hard.

Did I always make my intimate oneness with Jody my priority? No, but I worked hard at it. Still, I have a lot to learn.

So, as you ponder these Dangerous Questions, know that I'm pondering along with you. Yes, it might get a little uncomfortable as we look deeply within, but I promise you, you will also laugh and even have fun. My desire is to help you see how to live out your marriage, not by default, but by design.

So let's get started!

What Is Really Important to Me?

*The greatest thing in this world is not so much where
we are, but in what direction we are moving.*
Oliver Wendell Holmes

*There are four steps to accomplishment: Plan purposefully.
Prepare prayerfully. Proceed Positively. Pursue Persistently.*
Author Unknown

*Marriage is not simply the luck of the draw, or something
that we get involved in which just unfolds before us like
a long movie. Good marriage, like good individual lives
or good art, are conscious creations. They are made.*
Kevin and Marilyn Ryan, *Blessing Your Husband*

Insight 1: WHAT DO MY CHOICES SAY?

Some couples have low-maintenance marriages, some medium-, and others high-maintenance marriages. Mine has been of the high variety. My wonderful husband, Jody, and I are not just different—we are wildly different. Jody is an introvert, I'm an extrovert. Jody is a thinker, I am a feeler.

Jody, Mr. Flow with It, dislikes plans. Plans give me a sense of security, and I love structure.

I remember a road trip from Vienna, Austria, to Katawice, Poland. When I plan a trip, I have maps, contact numbers, and backup contact numbers. When Jody plans a trip, he does "whatever." As we were driving toward Poland, I asked the "whatever" man where he put the map. He had no map. To clarify, this trip was taken when Poland was still under Communist rule, and road signs were either nonexistent or incomprehensible. A map was a necessity. But we had no map.

I started to fume inside.

We made it to Poland, and I asked Jody where he had put the directions to the hotel. No directions … and he wasn't sure which hotel it was … but he could find it. Now my insides were tangled inside out, and I wanted very much to say everything I was thinking, but I was sure that when he couldn't find the hotel, he would see that planning was the best way to travel. Jody found the hotel in half an hour. Sometimes, life just isn't fair.

Over the years, my "whatever" husband has graciously learned to bring maps and other information to help me feel more comfortable.

Jody is an entrepreneur and lives in the future. I live for today and think practically how to make today work. I followed this man I'm married to from the United States to Europe, where we lived for fourteen years. From Europe we moved to Asia for three years and then back to the States. Jody has a new plan every day, and with each new idea, I feel sick to my stomach. Which country is next on his world tour?

Because Jody and I are from different planets, growing in intimate oneness has not been easy. It has taken lots of adapting, lots of accepting, and lots of forgiving. It has also meant paying attention to the choices I make.

When we had three children and the oldest was just three, we lived in Dallas, Texas. There were days I was so tired, I couldn't think. Our youngest had asthma, and many nights I slept on a thin mattress next to his bed.

When he woke unable to breathe at 3:00 a.m. it was a rush into the bathroom turned into a steam cave or a rush to the emergency room.

One day I realized that my choices said something about what was important to me. I started asking myself what message my choices said to Jody about how important he was to me. What message did Jody get from me? Did I walk away from him and say, "Don't even think about sex or a good meal. Can't you see I'm wiped out?" Or did I walk toward him, put my arms around him, and whisper, "I can't wait until life is easier and I can spend a day loving you"? What attitude did I project? What atmosphere did I create? What did my choices say was really most important to me? Sometimes what is most important to us is not obvious and can be seen only by how we respond to our husbands in everyday life.

When four teens roamed our home, we lived in Vienna, Austria. Life was filled with soccer, track, volleyball, ski team, musicals, boyfriends, girlfriends, and so much more. Jody traveled on long trips to Communist Eastern Europe. When he was gone, the boys and I were on coal-furnace duty. That thing hated me—no matter what I did, it went out. I can't count the times I cried over the coal furnace. What message did I give Jody when he arrived home after a long and dangerous trip? Did I run into his arms and indicate I couldn't wait until later, or did I gripe and complain about the coal furnace and every little thing that had gone wrong with the house, kids, and life during the month he was traveling? What did my behavior say was most important to me?

Now we live in Monument, Colorado, and the house is quiet. Only Bailey, our big golden retriever, is here to make noise and create a mess. So … now it is easy to make Jody a priority, right? Wrong. Exciting ministry, precious women's problems, and just plain-old life get in the way. If it isn't little children, teens, a friend in need, or a demanding job, it is illness, a broken-down car, or a bear break-in. The list goes on.… One thing is clear:

My choices must say that Jody is my first priority of all the people on earth.

I remember a time I did this right. Jody and I were leaving for a five-day celebration of our thirteenth anniversary in the Arkansas mountains. Visions of deep communication and romantic walks by the river filled my head. It was going to be wonderful. The children were parceled out to friends' houses. While I had gone to the store to get a few last-minute things for the trip, Jody tried to fix the leak in the bathroom. And the drip, instead of diminishing, turned into a gush that became a flood.

Returning home from the store, I walked into a world of water-soaked carpets, neighbors madly mopping and scooping water. It was a water-logged nightmare. I vacuumed carpets with a water vacuum, pulled carpets up and hung them over the fence. Jody emptied our water bed of water so we could get the water-soaked carpet out from under the bed and over the fence to drip-dry. The final blow came while moving furniture in the bedroom. My wedding ring, which had been on the dresser, was lost. This was my anniversary, and I didn't even have a wedding ring. Instead of taking a romantic walk by the river, I walked around the house with a flashlight, tears streaming down my face, looking in every nook and cranny for my ring, but no ring was to be found.

Early the next morning, I was ready for action. First the ring, then the soggy carpets. Before I could put my planning into gear, Jody made an incredible statement, the kind of statement that only a man can make. "Honey, let's just forget all this mess, bring the carpets in off the fence, pile them in the living room, and head for the mountains. We still have four days left of our vacation trip." I looked at the waterlogged house and then in amazement at my man. He really meant it! How could I just leave the mess and forget it?

At this point, the last thing I wanted was a romantic walk by the river. I wanted to find my wedding ring and salvage my carpets. My feelings screamed, "No, I can't go," so I took my feelings and my will to the bathroom, locked the door, sat on the closed potty, and prayed.

Lord, You know how I feel; I don't want to be alone with my husband. All I can think about is my stale, smelling house and my wrinkled carpets. But, Lord, my husband has said "let's go," and I know he's right. There will always be a reason why it's not a good time to escape. This time the reason just seems very big, but I choose in my will to go with my husband. I choose to forget the mess. I trust You to change my feelings.

The five-hour ride to the Arkansas mountains remains clear in my memory, because it was a five-hour battle between my feelings and my will. Every ten minutes, I started to think about my lost ring, the soggy carpets, and the mess. Each time I had to choose to reject the thoughts and concentrate on my husband. Gradually, and I do mean gradually, my feelings went along with the choices in my will.

By the time we arrived at our hideaway, we had three days left. How do I describe those thirty-six hours? There truly are no words to relate the beautiful, deep intimacy that we experienced. The depth of our communication amazed me. We sensed a more profound oneness between us, and we even had a romantic walk by the river.

I have always believed that God rewarded me with those beautiful hours because I made a secret choice to let Jody know he was important to me when my feelings were screaming, "I can't walk away from this muggy mess!"

Often I ask myself, *Will I be happy with my choice five years from now or twenty years in the future?* My choice to leave the waterlogged disaster and *go* with my husband was thirty-four years ago. Yes, I am happy—oh, so thankful—that I chose to make my husband my priority and to put my marriage first. That is what is really important.

P.S. Seven years after the notorious Dillow Flood, the couple renting our house found my lost ring. Jody saved it and gave it to me on our twentieth wedding anniversary.

Insight 2: MARRIAGE MATTERS

Think back for a moment to your marriage, the day you entered into a sacred covenant with your husband before God. When you floated down the aisle wearing white, ready to have that ring on your finger and that man as yours alone, you likely weren't thinking about marriage as a sacred covenant. I sure wasn't! My mind was centered more on thoughts of being "naked with no guilty feelings"! But God was thinking about this special union at your wedding and mine. To Him, marriage is the most sacred commitment between two people.

In modern language, a covenant signifies that two people have become one. Look with me at how God defines marriage in the book of Genesis:

> *For this reason a man will leave his father and mother and be united to his wife, and they will become one flesh. (2:24 NIV)*

Moses wrote down this scripture as part of the Torah, the Hebrew Scriptures long before it was called Genesis. The Israelites, like you and me, had less-than-perfect marriages, so God sent His prophets to remind them about the covenant they had made before God with their marriage partner. In this next passage, the Jewish people were weeping and wailing because God no longer paid attention to their offerings. They asked God, "Why don't you hear us?" God answered in Malachi 2:14–15:

> *It is because the LORD is acting as the witness between you and the wife of your youth, because you have broken faith with her, though she is your partner, the wife of your marriage covenant.*

> *Has not the LORD made them one? In flesh and spirit they are his.… So guard yourself in your spirit, and do not break faith with the wife of your youth. (NIV)*

My friend, if you were married by a minister of the gospel, you were saying, "There is a divine dimension to marriage, and we are making a covenant before God."

Marriage as a sacred covenant has two parts: something you do and something God does.

Your part: You agreed to exchange vows, pledges, that you will honor before God and others. God was also a witness as you made your solemn covenant commitment to each other.

God's part: After you declare your covenant promises, God then does something to you and your husband. He takes the two very different people, and in a beautiful and holy way, makes them one, one in flesh and one in spirit.

Jody and I recently attended a wedding where the bride and groom, Bethany and Chris, read the following vows, which they had each written:

> *I, Bethany, take you, Chris, to be my husband, to have and to hold, to respect and admire, to comfort and encourage. God has blessed me with a greater gift than I ever could have asked for or imagined, and that gift is you. I will strive throughout the good times and the bad times, to be your greatest cheerleader, to consistently affirm you and support you. I will prioritize and grow in my relationship with you and with the Lord. I promise to trust you. Where you go I will go, and where you stay I will stay. Your people will be my people, and your God will be my God. I commit to love and to cherish you from this day forward until death do us part.*

> *I, Chris, take you, Bethany, to be my wife. To have and to hold, to support, encourage, and protect as God's precious gift to me. You are—and always will be—my best friend, and I am so happy that from this day forward we will face all of life's joys and trials together. I will do my best to approach our marriage with gentleness, compassion, humility, openness, and grace. I will always*

*pursue God first and you second above all else. I promise to strive
to lead according to God's will and lean on His grace and love
as a perfect example of how I am to love you. You will always be
honored, appreciated, and safe in our marriage. I commit to love
and cherish you from now until death do us part.*

As I listened to these beautiful covenant promises to each other, I thought, *And now God does His part and begins to make them one.*

There is a holy reverence about the marriage covenant. Your marriage matters to God, and I believe it matters to you. My friend, you willingly vowed to bind yourself to this man you loved, and God supernaturally began to make you one. It is a glorious thing. I bow and worship and thank my God. He is an amazing Creator!

As you read Bethany and Chris's wedding vows, what were your thoughts? Did you think, *I remember being that young and in love, but it is gone … gone … gone. We are soooo far from that kind of love relationship at this point in our marriage. I wish I had the chance to do things over, to make different choices.*

If so, there is hope!

Insight 3: THE TREADMILL WON'T STOP!

When a friend's husband dies, you look with new eyes at your husband. Listen to these words from some friends of a grieving wife.… They speak volumes:

*The little things that used to be so big have all but faded away.
It's a lot easier to see and live in the broader picture, appreciat-
ing and savoring the moments we have. My life will never be the
same … and neither will my thankfulness that my husband is here
living it with me. I have such a longing to make sure I say what's
important—to communicate my heart of gratefulness to my husband and children.*

Watching my friend in such pain has brought an urgency about today—to not let things that have gone untended in our marriage go any longer. To take hard steps to fight for something better and even dream about having something wonderful again.

God has confirmed to me that my priorities are seriously out of whack, and how badly I need Him to help me truly make my marriage a priority.

When a husband dies, when divorce strikes someone close and children are weeping because Daddy's gone, when your friend can't stop crying because of her husband's affair, pain pushes you to remember that your husband is important. But the question is: *How do I keep my husband a priority in the chaos of everyday life? How do I get God's perspective in my brain and heart?*

Jesus didn't mince words about keeping first things first. He said, love God first and love your neighbor as yourself (Matt. 22:37–39). Simple and clear. So who is your closest neighbor? The one who shares your bed and daily bread: your husband.

Do I see you shaking your head and saying, "Linda, what planet do you live on? That might look good on paper, but it just doesn't fly in reality." If so, know you have lots of company. Many of the wives I've talked with feel stuck on the treadmill:

I work a stressful job and come home to kids, cooking, laundry, and a husband with needs. Everyone at home and work wants a piece of me.

I homeschool four children, my husband works from home, and I'm his accountant. If I step off the treadmill … oh, it's not possible.

If I'm really honest, the real truth is, I don't want to get off the treadmill. If life slows down, I'll have to look in the mirror—and Dangerous Questions? Not me!

Believe me, I understand. I had three children in three years, adopted a fourth when he was a teen, and had teenagers ages thirteen, fourteen, fifteen, and seventeen. I can still feel that overwhelming scatteredness that made my head spin. Children do that to you.

When life hammers us, priorities are smashed. While the notations on our calendars are unique to each of us, in one way we are all alike: We each must make a daily choice about what we will prioritize and about what must be demoted to a "do later" status. While it's easy to put our husbands on the back burner, it can be devastating to a marriage. In fact, when I asked women to tell me the worst thing they had done in their marriage, many of them said that it was not making their husband a priority. Here is a sampling of their responses:

I focus on other things in life; I don't take time for my marriage. I put more thought, energy, and effort into my relationship with our kids and grandkids than in my own husband and our relationship. (Married twenty-eight years)

I got too busy and had no time for my husband. I allowed my kids to take priority over my hubby. (Married seven years)

I have put my children first before my husband. (Married seventeen years)

I never think about my marriage. My life is a treadmill, and I can't stop running and think. I just move from one area of need to another. My children and job scream louder than my husband, so he gets left out. (Married fourteen years)

Is it just me, or do you also see a pattern in these answers? One woman said it well: "I don't always get it straight. I get caught up in the thick of thin things. What matters most—my walk with God and love affair with my husband—gets buried under layers of pressing problems and immediate concerns."

Are you on a treadmill? When was the last time you stopped long enough to think deeply about your marriage? I want to ask you to do something for me. STOP! Step off your treadmill, and find a quiet place to read the next few pages. I know, you're laughing because there isn't a quiet place. Then go in the bathroom, lock the door, put the lid down, and sit there.

When life is hectic, we don't stop and think about our priorities. We don't think about what is really important. We avoid looking within and reflecting. We neglect looking at God's Word and praying, *Search my heart, O God.* We mistakenly think that it is easier to stay busy. And truth be told, we like the way others see us when we're balancing five things at once. Friends say, "Cara is amazing. I just don't see how she does it all." That feels good—better than stepping off the treadmill and asking heart-wrenching Dangerous Questions.

Perhaps you're braver than that. Are you willing to look in the mirror and honestly ask, *What is* really *important to me?*

How can you gain perspective on your marriage relationship when life just won't stop? You must live with the end in view. Read on to find out more.

Insight 4: LIVE WITH THE END IN VIEW

I've been privileged, thus far, to have had forty-six years, five months, and twenty-six days with my lover and best friend. Living with the end in view means that I am aware of how I spend these hours, conscious that they are a gift, that there are only so many hours I have left, and that only God knows the number. It may be five years or fifty years. No matter how many years we have to grow in our intimate oneness, the time is short. When we realize this, *really realize it,* it can change the way we look at time, at love, and at our lover. Sadly, many wives discover too late the gift they possessed.

One such wife is seen in the Pulitzer Prize-winning drama *Our Town*. Emily, the young wife in the drama, had died at age twenty-six but was allowed the privilege of returning to an ordinary day from her earthly life. But with the opportunity, she was warned: "At least, choose an unimportant day. Choose the least important day in your life. It will be important enough."[1]

She chooses to relive her twelfth birthday, but soon she cries, "I can't. I can't go on. It goes so fast. We don't have time to look at one another. I didn't realize. So all that was going on and we never noticed."[2]

Another character comments from the grave.

> Yes.… That's what it was to be alive. To move about in a cloud of ignorance; to go up and down trampling on the feelings of those … about you. To spend and waste time as though you had a million years. To be always at the mercy of one self-centered passion, or another.[3]

But it is Emily's question that pierces the heart: "Do any human beings ever realize life while they live it?"[4] The answer given is no.

We're encouraged in the Scriptures not to move about in ignorance, not to waste time as if we had a million years, but to realize life is short.

> Teach us to number our days and recognize how few they are; help us to spend them as we should. (Ps. 90:12 TLB).

> Live life then, with a due sense of responsibility, not as [women] who do not know the meaning and purpose of life but as those who do. Make the best use of your time, despite all the evils of these days. Don't be vague but firmly grasp what you know to be the will of the Lord. (Eph. 5:15–16 PH)

I've often thought that if we knew exactly how many hours, days, years we had together, we might be more aware of how important each choice we make is. But God has not chosen to let us know. At the end of his life, the apostle Paul was able to say, "I have fought the good fight, I have finished the race.… Now there is in store for me the crown of righteousness" (2 Tim. 4:7–8 NIV). Too often a woman approaches the end of life and inwardly laments, *I've fought a mediocre fight as a wife. I didn't run well in my race.*

I want to be a woman of focus. I don't want to live by default, but by design. So, how do I begin to live by design? I go to the Designer and pray:

> *Lord, You created me, You created my husband. You gave us our personalities, our strengths and weaknesses. You know us both intimately. You see exactly how we can mesh together, glorify You, and enjoy each other. So, God, it feels scary, but I'm going to be brave; I'm willing to think about me as a wife. I'll even reflect on this Dangerous Question: What is it like to be married to me?*

I want to take you on a journey with me, a journey through your life as a wife; I want to help you live your marriage backwards.

To help you live with the end in view, I want to take you to a funeral. Now don't put down the book. I assure you that I have not lost my mind and that I know what I'm doing.

In your mind's eye, visualize yourself going to the funeral of a loved one.[5] Picture yourself driving to the church, parking the car, and getting out. As you enter the sanctuary, you hear your favorite worship song being played, you see the faces of friends and family and feel the sorrow of loss and the joy of having known that is so evident on their faces. As you walk to the front of the church and look inside the casket, you come face-to-face with yourself. With disbelief, you realize that this is your funeral, thirty years from today. The people gathered together are here to express their love and appreciation for your life. Numb with shock, you are led to a seat and handed a program.

You look at the program in your hand and see that there is to be a speaker, your husband. Now think long and hard.

- What would you like your husband to say about you after many years of marriage?
- What character qualities would you like him to have seen in you?
- What kind of love relationship would you want him to describe?
- What kind of love would you have wanted him to have received from you during all those years?

As you think deeply about these questions, write down your thoughts and feelings. This exercise will reveal to you what your deepest values are, who you want to become as a wife. To live your life with the end in view is to align your daily and secret choices with this picture. It is to examine each part of your life—what you do today, tomorrow, next week, next year; how you chose to spend the time with your lover—in the context of the whole, of what really matters most to you.

When you are at the beginning of something, it is very difficult to think about its end. I'm headed toward the home stretch of my marriage, and it's still difficult to have this perspective. We are "daily" people, not life-time people, but God wants us to be eternal people. How I wish someone had asked me to visualize my funeral at the beginning of my marriage. This thought process helps put all we hope and desire into perspective. Don't move on until you have completed this exercise, and be sure to keep what you write so that you can refer to it later.

Insight 5: AIM FOR THE GOAL

Kathy is a woman of focus, purposeful about her role as a mom, in her job, in her ministry. She has goals for every area of her life—except her marriage. I sent her this Dangerous Question to critique as I was writing the book. She responded by email.

Hey Coach Linda,

I'm sitting here in tears. This was waaaaay tougher than I thought it would be. I mean, I'm a life coach, "coaching" women about their purpose in life. And you know that I have goals for every area of my own life—but I've never thought about a marriage goal. Hello???

This assignment really made me focus on Scott ... and on my marriage. Marriage really is an "our" thing, isn't it? Hearing what he may say about me as a wife when I'm "gone" was a gut-wrenching exercise. Thanks, once again, for making me think.

Your mentee,
Kathy

Have you ever thought about your goals as a wife? If you want to spend your days with the end in view, you need to take what you wrote about what you want your husband to say at your funeral and change those thoughts into goals. Keep in mind that there is a difference between a goal and a desire. That alone will have a tremendous effect on your level of contentedness in marriage.

Sarah learned this the hard way. She had a goal for her marriage: to have an intimate oneness, a close, wonderful relationship with her husband, Sam. Being a young woman of purpose and commitment to Christ, she read every book on sex, on communication in marriage, attended seminars on being a wife, and worked hard to create intimacy with her husband.

But after five years of marriage, Sarah was angry, frustrated, and disillusioned. She felt that her marriage was a farce. She'd tried so hard to communicate, but Sam, the strong, silent type, simply grew more silent. The more she talked about closeness, the more he retreated. Without realizing what she was doing, Sarah gradually spent her hours and days devising plans to change "silent Sam" into "sharing Sam." The more she demanded an intimate oneness, the more she and Sam grew into two separate people with a chasm between them.

My heart ached for Sarah. She desperately desired intimate closeness with Sam, and God desired it as well. After all, He is the One who said, "The two shall become one." Sarah's motives were right, but her goal was wrong, and this was the cause of her anger and disillusionment.

Are you saying, "Wait a minute, Linda—Sarah's goal was in alignment with God's purpose for marriage, so how can it be wrong?" If so, I understand. It's easy to confuse our goals and our desires. I once had my goals and desires mixed up too.

So, what is a goal?

A *goal* is a purpose to which a woman is unalterably committed.[6] She assumes unconditional responsibility for a goal, and it can be achieved if she is willing to work at it.

A *desire* is something wanted that cannot be obtained without the cooperation of another person. It is an objective for which a person can assume no responsibility because it is beyond her control. Reaching a desire must never become the motivating purpose behind behavior, because then a person is assuming responsibility for something she cannot fulfill on her own.

A goal is something I want that I can also control.

A desire is something I want that I cannot control.

If I desire to lose weight, I can make it my goal, because I am responsible for what I eat and whether I exercise. But if I desire my husband to lose weight, it does no good to put a tiny chicken breast and three stalks of broccoli on his plate. I can't make his weight my goal because I can't control another person's eating or exercise. Women who try to get their husbands to lose weight by programming their eating only end up angering their husbands and feeling frustrated and unhappy when their "goal" is not achieved. I polled several wives, asking, "What is your goal for your marriage?" The responses were similar to Sarah's:

To have an exciting, romantic relationship.

To have a wonderful marriage.

To have my marriage be a picture of Christ's love.

To develop a deep intimacy in all areas of our marriages.

Each of these goals sounds positive, even lofty. They are good goals to have, right? Sorry, wrong. Go back to the definition of a goal. My goal for my marriage has to be something I can control, something I can work toward. One of the most important things to learn in life and love is that I can be responsible only for what I can control. While I can't control my husband (or anyone else), I can control me.

Sarah's anger and frustration came because she couldn't control her husband, Sam. He wouldn't do *his* part to bring about a wonderful openness and intimacy in their marriage. Sarah's goal—to have an intimate oneness, a close, wonderful relationship with her husband—could only be a desire, not a goal. To be achievable, our goals for our marriage must be things we are responsible for and can control. So, a legitimate goal for Sarah would be for her to do her part to bring about intimacy in her marriage.

I know you join me in saying that every husband should do his part to have a lover and best-friend relationship with his spouse, to be everything that God has commanded him to be as a husband. But that is a choice a husband makes before God. We can't force our husbands to do these things, nor should we try to nag or manipulate. We cannot control them into doing these. God must motivate your husband. A wife can do things to invite her husband into deeper intimacy, but ultimately she must entrust her man to Him.

Recently, I found some notes, written years ago. At that time I was trying to discover why I was frustrated when I'd worked so hard at being a loving wife. Here is what I wrote in the wee hours of the morning:

> *My goal can only be to be a godly wife. My desire and earnest prayer—to have a wonderful marriage. I am responsible for me. I am not responsible for Jody. I can't be responsible for what I can't control, and I certainly cannot control my husband. BUT I can control me, or better stated, I can learn to control me. I can learn, with God's power and motivation, to daily make the choices that will lead me toward my goal of being a godly wife.*

So, my friend, you and I can make it a goal to be a godly wife. We can make it a goal to be as open and intimate with our husband as possible. Let's work toward our goals, and pray for the things we desire for our marriages.

Insight 6: GET A VISION FOR YOUR MARRIAGE

It's time to get practical. You've visualized your funeral and thought deeply about who you want to become as a wife. We've discussed the difference between a desire and a goal. Now, I want to help you write a personal Marriage Purpose Statement. A Marriage Purpose Statement is your conscious creation of who you want to become. It outlines your goals as a wife—the things you can do to become the wife you want to be. Like a rudder on a ship, it steers your marriage boat, so that you know where you are heading. Your personal Marriage Purpose Statement can be a letter you write to yourself, a prayer, a poem, a verse, or a passage of Scripture. It can be anything that declares your goals for your marriage. It is a statement about what is *really* important to you as a wife.

I asked the women in my pilot Bible studies to read these pages and to visualize their own funerals. Once they had identified what they wanted their husbands to say about them, I had them articulate the kind of wife they wanted to be and become by writing their own personal Marriage Purpose Statement.

Kathy wrote the following poem as her Marriage Purpose Statement.

Echoes

The gap so wide, the canyon so deep
I can barely see the other side
From the wife I am to who I desire to be
What bridges this great divide?

The sound of His voice on that distant day
Makes me stop and rethink my steps
Will he be a better man for the choices I've made?
Will he rejoice in the vows I've kept?

How can he see you in the home we make
Living from day to day
As this wife looks ahead to the end of our time
What would I want my husband to say?

"She was patient and kind
Mindful of our time
She was faithful, trustworthy and honest
She forgave and sought my heart

Was attentive to my needs
She encouraged me to lead

"She was playful and fun
Her smile like the sun
She was my comforter, lover, and friend
She persevered, believed the truth
Saw dreams I couldn't see
She found the best in me

"Lord, I thank You for this woman
Who fought for this man
She prayed and never stopped
She cherished me body, mind, and soul
Deeper than I ever knew
Her love led me to You."

Words echo in the canyon, tears pool in my eyes
Can I ever become this wife?
Can my actions speak without a word
To tell of everlasting life?

I desire to become the wife of his dreams
While uniquely walking this course
Your Word spans the distance across this divide
Your truth is my constant source.[7]

Jossie, a young mom with four little ones, used her husband's name, Aaron, as the basis for her Marriage Purpose Statement. She said that she uses her husband's name a lot and that having his name in her statement would help her think about it often. She wrote:

I will be:

Attentive to Aaron, our friendship, romance, partnership in parenting, and to the state of our marriage.

I will:

Admire and appreciate who he is, all he contributes, and ways he is growing/being challenged in life.

I will take:

Responsibility for my attitudes and approach to life in submission to the Lord and partnership with Aaron.

I will remain:

Open to growing, learning, and investing and to the Holy Spirit as He leads us.

I will draw:

Near to God and Aaron as we navigate each day and every season.

Alice wrote her Marriage Purpose Statement as a prayer based on Philippians 4:8–9:

Lord, I want to fix my eyes on everything about Gary that is true and honorable and right because Gary IS an honorable man. I want to think and act admirably, pure, and lovely and make a peaceful home for him. I want to be a woman who is excellent and worthy of praise because he deserves no less. I want to put these things into practice—wrapped up with love and infused with a generous supply of humor, adventure, and fun. I want to keep learning and working and trying to be God's best so that God's peace will be a hedge of protection around our home, our lives, and our hearts.

Let me close by sharing with you my personal Marriage Purpose Statement. It is an acrostic of the word *faithful,* followed by declarative statements.

My marriage matters to God and to me, so I choose to be:

F	A	I	T	H	F	U	L
o	t	n	h	e	o	n	a
c	t	t	a	l	r	w	s
u	i	i	n	p	g	a	t
s	t	m	k	e	i	v	i
	u	a	f	r	v	e	n
	d	c	u		i	r	g
	e	y	l		n	i	
					g	n	
						g	

I choose to	*Focus.*
I choose a positive	*Attitude.*
I choose deep	*Intimacy.*
I choose to be	*Thankful.*
I choose to be a	*Helper.*
I choose to be	*Forgiving.*
I choose to be	*Unwavering.*
I choose a	*Lasting marriage.*

As I write, it is so evident to me that I still have a long way to go in becoming the wife God desires me to be and that I long to be, but I realize also that because I have made these commitments before the Lord, I am much farther down the path of becoming that wife.

It is time for you to reflect, think, pray, and write your own Marriage Purpose Statement. Find a quiet place (this will be the hardest step). Get out the notes you took when you thought about what you would want your husband to say about you at your funeral. These words describe who you hope to become. It's time to turn them into goals.

Your personal Marriage Purpose Statement can be a:

- Resolution or declaration
- Prayer
- Scripture
- Poem or song
- Letter you write to yourself
- Acrostic
- List or paragraph

Your Marriage Purpose Statement doesn't have to sound beautiful or be perfect in any way. This is a personal commitment between you and God, something for you to keep in the forefront of your mind, to pray about often, to use as a thermometer when you are taking your "wife temperature." It is something to go back to and reflect on each anniversary when you thank God for your husband and for the growth in your life and relationship during the preceding year.

Now that you have reflected on what is really important to you and written down who you want to become, you are on your way to being a wife, not by default but by design.

Dangerous Prayer!

Lord, You are showing me what is really important to me. Please help me stop being a wife by default. I want to become a wife by design!

What Does It Feel Like to Be My Husband?

A new Perfect Husband Shopping Center opened where a woman could go to choose from among many men to find the perfect husband. It was laid out on five floors, with the men increasing in positive attributes as you ascended the floors. The only rule was that once you open the door to any floor, you must choose a man from that floor, and if you go up a floor, you can't go back down except to leave the store. So, two girlfriends go to the store to find a man to marry.

> The first-floor sign reads: "These men have high-paying jobs and love kids."
>
> The women read the sign and say, "Well, that's wonderful! ... But I wonder what's on the next floor."
>
> The second-floor sign reads: "These men have high-paying jobs, love kids, and are extremely good looking."
>
> "Hmmm," say the girls. "What's further up?"
>
> The third-floor sign reads: "These men have high-paying jobs, love kids, are extremely good looking, and will help with the housework."
>
> "Wow!" say the women. "Very tempting, but there's more further up!"

The fourth-floor sign reads: "These men have high-paying jobs, love kids, are extremely good looking, will help with house-work, and are great in bed!"

"Oh, mercy me. But just think! What must be awaiting us further up?!" say the women.

So, up to the fifth floor they go.

The fifth-floor sign reads: "This floor is just to prove that women are impossible to please."[1]

Insight 1: SOPHISTICATED VENTING

When Dr. Laura Schlessinger surveyed husbands for her book *The Proper Care and Feeding of Husbands*, she learned that the universal complaint of men was that their wives criticize, complain, nag, rarely compliment or express appreciation, are difficult to satisfy, and basically are not as nice to them as they'd be to a stranger ringing their doorbell at 3:00 a.m.

Listen to what one husband said about how his wife made him feel:

> *At work I have always had superlative evaluations on my performance. AT HOME I CAN'T DO ANYTHING RIGHT! I sometimes spend several minutes in thought on a task at hand, trying to decide exactly what to do. After weighing the pros and cons, I make a decision and act. Almost invariably I get, "What did you do that for? Now I can't …," or I hear, "Who put the ??? here," or sometimes I get a straight-out "That's stupid." … It is something that wears you down like erosion.*[2]

I personally talked to a sad husband who said this about his wife:

> *My wife is always depressed and negative, and her complaining gets to me. One day I found myself following a lovely, laughing*

*woman around Walmart—I was embarrassed, but it just felt good
to be around a happy, positive woman.*

Lest you think, *I'm not that bad,* I wonder what would your husband say?

A few years ago, Jody and I were involved in a project surveying five hundred Christian couples. The husbands were asked, "What is the one thing you would most like to have in a wife?" Surprisingly, the majority answered, "A positive attitude about life." So, these five hundred men wanted just what the men in Dr. Laura's survey wanted—wives who encouraged them.

Some wives are unaware that they are gold-medal gripers. This was true of Reba. She went to her pastor with pages of complaints against her husband. After hours of uninterrupted listening, he couldn't help but ask, "If your husband is that bad, why did you marry him?" Immediately the wife replied, "He wasn't like this at first." The pastor had to ask, "So are you saying that he is like this because he's been married to you?"[3]

I know, not funny. But the pastor has a point. How did Reba change from a dreamy-eyed bride to a nagging wife with pages of complaints against her husband? Did she make choices that turned her into a griping wife?

The book of Proverbs says, "A wise woman builds her home, but a foolish woman tears it down with her own hands" (14:1 NLT). How does a wife tear down and destroy her man? Oh, there are overt ways, but some of us are really good at what I call *sophisticated venting.*

Listen to one woman's comments about how some women act when they get together.

*The women's group was not the help I'd been hoping for.... [T]he
group was a gripe session for women to vent about their husbands'
idiosyncrasies, bad attitudes, and failures in general and in specific. I was becoming trained to complain and whine about real*

or imagined behavior and look for sympathy from other women. I discontinued participation.[4]

A young friend relayed the following story to me: "I was waiting at the elementary school for my kids to get out and saw two women I knew, so I walked up to them. I could hear them venting about their husbands long before I reached them. Knowing that I had heard their caustic gripes, one laughingly said, 'Oh, this is just what we do!'"

Two Christian women think it is a joke to rag on their husbands. That's just not funny.

The hundreds of women involved in my survey believed that attitude is a Big Deal. In fact, many felt that the worst thing they did for their marriages was to have a crummy attitude. Listen to their comments.

I took my husband for granted. He gets the worst part of me on my bad days and what's left of me most days. (Married thirty-four years)

Nagging. Trying to make my husband who I want him to be. (Married ten years)

My glass is always half-empty. I have been the wet blanket that has held him back from some of his dreams. (Married forty years)

I criticize my husband on a daily basis. (Married seventeen years)

I always complain about where we live. My husband has a wonderful job, and I know my grumbling and ingratitude has hurt him. (Married seventeen years)

Just being an old nag about his smoking, and you know what, I might as well shut up as it is killing me to be a nag. (Married a long time)

Thinking about what I don't have in a husband instead of working on being the best wife. (Married eleven years)

How do you respond when you read about grumbling, griping, nagging, venting, complaining wives?

Do you think:

I'm not like that! I'm a positive person.

Or do you think:

If you were married to my husband, you'd gripe too!

Many of the wives I talk with believe that adultery, drinking too much, abusing prescription drugs, using four-letter words—even gossip—is wrong. But griping? "Linda, life is hard; complaining is just part of life."

I often hear statements like these:

My attitude just happens. I have no control over it.

I deserve to be able to gripe.

Griping isn't so bad.

I find that most Christian women think it is okay to whine and complain, now and then. Problem is, now and then turns into daily routine.

Let me balance this picture by saying that I know many incredible wives whose husbands feel loved and appreciated. You may be like them and bring delight to your unique man. Or you may fall somewhere in between.

No matter where you fall on the griping spectrum, I feel certain you don't want your husband to think, *I can't do anything right.* None of us wants our husband following strange women around Walmart just because they want to be in the presence of a positive woman. God will help you honestly answer the Dangerous Question: *What does it feel like to be my husband?*

All of us can benefit from understanding why we are so prone to grip-ing, so let's explore that next.

Insight 2: WHERE DID I CATCH THE GRIPING DISEASE?

Barbara Johnson, author of many books, could make anything funny. I think you'll agree with me that lots of wives would vent about Bill's idea of what qualifies as a creative gift.

> *In most marriages, husbands and wives eventually adapt to each other's differences, no matter how eccentric they are. One of the things I've had to adapt to is that Bill is very frugal (TIGHT is the word!). For instance, sometime back when my publisher noti-fied us that sales of my books had reached the one million mark, Bill said we ought to celebrate. He got in the car and disappeared for a while, and I imagined him arranging some quiet little din-ner party at a fancy restaurant or even shopping for some special gift for me. Jewelry would be nice, I thought.*
>
> *Instead he came home, smiling broadly, with two bunches of fresh asparagus! "I know how much you love it," he said as he dropped his gift into the kitchen sink. Hardly my way of celebrating!*[5]

Perhaps you think, *Getting asparagus as a gift—that's nothing to gripe about. That's a piece of cake compared to my life.* You may be right. No one knows what happens inside your marriage but you. Even so, your husband is not the cause of your griping. You didn't catch the griping disease from him.

Joyce Meyer believes that your thinking patterns gave you the disease. She writes:

> *Thinking about what you're thinking about is very valuable because Satan usually deceives [women] into thinking that the source of their misery or trouble is something other than what it*

really is. He wants them to think they are unhappy due to what is going on around them (their [husbands]), but the misery is actually due to what is going on inside them (their thoughts).[6]

God's Word validates Joyce Meyer's words. The message of Proverbs 23:7 is: You are going to become what you dwell on. We become what we think. Yikes! That's scary!

It's much like GIGO. If you are a computer whiz, you know this acronym. For those who are not, let me explain. GIGO means "garbage in, garbage out." Computer programmers know that whatever they feed into a computer will inevitably show up in the printouts. So if garbage goes in, garbage will come out.

Your brain is a fabulous computer, capable of recording eight hundred memories per second for seventy-five years without ever getting tired.[7] Amazing! God's Word says that what you feed into your mind will come out in your life (Prov. 23:7). So, if you go to a Sophisticated Venting Club and train your mind to think negative thoughts about your husband, if you meditate on all you don't like about him, if you fill your mind and heart with garbage about your man, garbage will be printed out—gripe, grumble, murmur, and vent will fill the pages of your life.

The often-quoted verse Philippians 4:8 commands us to think and mediate, not on garbage, but on all the positive, commendable, excellent, and praiseworthy qualities in others—and "others" includes husbands:

> *Finally, brethren, whatever is true, whatever is honorable, whatever is right, whatever is pure, whatever is lovely, whatever is of good repute, if there is any excellence and if anything worthy of praise, dwell on these things.*

The tragedy is that oh, so many wives have retranslated this precious verse, and their revised translation goes like this:

> *Finally, my sisters, concerning your husband, if there is anything*
> *that is untrue or dishonorable, if you can find an action that is*
> *not right, a thought that is impure, if you see anything unlovely*
> *(a receding hairline or potbelly), if anything about his work or*
> *habits is not commendable, if you can think of one thing about*
> *him that is not excellent or praiseworthy, dwell on these things.*
> *Reflect on them, chew them over, and mediate on them. Stir the*
> *pot of negative thinking about your man, and the god of griping*
> *and discontent will be with you.*

That was Jean's mantra, until a comment from one of her kids brought her up short and showed just how negative her attitude toward her husband had become. According to Jean, their married life was blissful until their fourth child was born and her husband, Jack, began a business. They had no automatic appliances or air-conditioning. Cooking really meant cooking, and most of the family responsibilities fell to Jean. Jack's schedule was nonexistent. He had to be at the store six days a week, all day long. One evening, he came home even later than normal, and as usual Jean started into her whining and griping. "Why are you so late *again?* Why can't you ever be on time for dinner?" You name it, Jean said it. Then one of her kids looked at her and said, "Mommy, why are you always mad at Daddy?"

God worked in her heart when she heard those words. Almost immediately the Holy Spirit spoke to her: *When you stand before your heavenly Father, He will not ask you about Jack's weaknesses, but He will ask you about your attitude of acceptance.*

She prayed, *God, do You mean that even though he interrupts my schedule and upsets our family, I'm supposed to be loving and kind and supportive?*

She said, "The Holy Spirit answered me sweetly, 'Yes, Jean.' … I had received a rebuke from the Lord and [knew] it was my responsibility to make things right."[8]

Jean's child's guileless words and the Holy Spirit's YES pushed her to begin to change. Jean wrote about this encounter when she had been married sixty years, which was long after it had happened. But she never forgot the lesson. God helped her learn to stop thinking of herself and her rights, and to be more sensitive to how her husband felt—and to how she could encourage rather than discourage him. She realized that only God can change the behavior of another, and when we point our finger at our husbands' shortcomings, three fingers are pointing back at us.

But Jean is unique among Christian wives. As I've said, most seem to think it is okay to whine and complain, at least now and then. So, we need to ask, what does God think about our "sometimes griping is okay" mentality?

Insight 3: GOD—ON GRIPING

God is the One we look to for wisdom about everything in our lives. What does He say about griping and what it does to us? I think you'll find His answer as we look at the two kinds of wives described in the book of Proverbs:

The Nag

> *A quarrelsome wife is as annoying*
> *as constant dripping on a rainy day.*
> *Stopping her complaints is like trying to stop the wind*
> *or trying to hold something with greased hands. (Prov.*
> *27:15–16 NLT)*

> *It's better to live alone in the corner of an attic*
> *than with a quarrelsome wife in a lovely home. (Prov. 25:24*
> *NLT)*

The Crown

An excellent wife is the crown of her husband,
*   But she who shames him is like rottenness in his bones.*
*   (Prov. 12:4)*

Her husband can trust her,
*   and she will greatly enrich his life.*
She brings him good, not harm,
*   all the days of her life. (Prov. 31:11–12 NLT)*

My friend Lorraine read these labels and said, "Some of us think we are nags with a crown on our heads!" Sadly, God mentions no crowned nags in Proverbs.

One thing about our Lord God—He is descriptive. And in these passages, He's black and white. No room for gray here! Either you're so impossible to live with that your husband camps out in a corner of the cold, dreary attic just to find a little peace, or you do him only good and enrich his life.

I have studied the book of Proverbs, and I see in its pages what I call "gender sins." A gender sin is a wrongful action or attitude commonly displayed by one gender as opposed to the other. *Gender sin* may not be in the dictionary, but Proverbs attributes "anger sin" to men and "nag sin" to women. Of course, wives get angry and husbands gripe, but every time Proverbs mentions a nagging, grumbling, contentious person, it is a married woman, a wife.

Clearly, God thinks it is bad to grumble—to gripe, bellyache, and complain. In fact, Scripture often points to people who failed God. Here's an example: In his first letter to the Corinthian believers, Paul reminds them about all the wonderful ways God demonstrated His power and faithfulness to the Israelites in the wilderness. They were guided by a cloud and by fire. God parted the Red Sea so the waves stood up like towers, and they walked across the Red Sea on dry ground. Amazing! Miraculous provisions! Yet Scripture says God was not pleased with the Israelites. Why? Three reasons: They were idolaters, they tested God, and they grumbled (1 Cor. 10:1–13).

This last reason caused me to have a little talk with God. Our discussion went something like this:

> *Linda: Wait a minute, God. Are You putting grumbling alongside immorality? Saying griping is as bad as adultery? Surely not!*
>
> *God: Yes, Linda, that is exactly what I am saying.*
>
> *Linda: That is really hard.*
>
> *God: Yes, it is. Linda, do you love Me?*
>
> *Linda: Lord, You know I love You.*
>
> *God: Do you remember what I said in 1 John 5:3? Loving Me means keeping My commandments.*
>
> *Linda: I get it, God. To You, griping is sin.*
>
> *God: You got it.*

God is against griping. He was not pleased when the Israelites complained in the wilderness. The apostle Paul tells us that what happened to them is a warning to us: "And do not grumble, as some of them did—and were killed by the destroying angel. These things happened to them as examples and were written down as warnings for us" (1 Cor. 10:10–11 NIV).

The Israelites' journey seemed unending; it was hot, and no one knew how many years this tedious desert walk would last. They became impatient and depressed because of the fierce trials along the way. And what did they do? They grumbled, griped, and complained to Moses—and also to God. Listen to their whining: "Why have you [God] brought us up out of Egypt to die in the desert? There is no bread! There is no water! And we detest this miserable food!" (Num. 21:5 NIV). (Yes, this was the miracle manna that they had earlier thanked God for sending from heaven.)

God is serious about grumbling. He says, "Do everything without complaining and arguing, so that no one can criticize you" (Phil. 2:14–15 NLT).

So, what prompts us to grumble and gripe? What prompts you? Is it because of the loss of income or a job? An overwhelming house payment? Having too many children? Not having any children? Or do your gripes center on your husband?

I've never met a woman who got married to be miserable. I married because I couldn't live without Jody Dillow, and I suspect you married because you couldn't imagine life without your husband either. But as the years pass, there are days when "the man I couldn't live without" becomes impossible to live with. The weaknesses that paled beside his glorious strengths now blare so loudly that his strengths are silenced.

When we vent, we often tell ourselves, *I am directing my complaints at this man who is so hard to live with,* but we are really griping to God. Our complaints say to God, "I know, Lord, that I asked You for this man, but I didn't know! I didn't know what it would be like to be married to him year after year after year. Yes, I thanked You for bringing us together. It seemed like a miracle then, but now, this husband You gave me is _____." (You fill in the blank.)

When we spend year after year dwelling on our husband's negative qualities and complaining about him to God (and to him and others), we can end up like this woman, who wrote:

I haven't made him happy at all. He never achieved his marvelous potential, even though he was an air force pilot, rose to a high rank, and earned a PhD. He has potential for greatness, but I stifled it. (Married fifty years)

When I read this comment on my survey, I felt like crying.

My friend, how is your attitude? Are you a "nag" like this woman or a "crown" like my friend Ruth?

I asked Ruth, who has been married for fifty years to Dr. Earl Radmacher, to take my survey. She went to her husband and asked him to describe the worst thing she had done for their marriage. His answer? "I can't think of any worst thing you've done." This made me smile. Ruth is her husband's crown.

You can be too.

Insight 4: GRIPES BE GONE!

You may be married to a man who is consistently thoughtful and kind, tenderly attentive to your needs. Yours is the model husband, amazingly unselfish and purposely helpful. If so, I hope you don't take him for granted. I hope you thank God—and your husband—daily.

But most of us live with an imperfect husband. What do we do with our complaints? Let's look at some spiritual and practical ways that have helped me make gripes be gone. My prayer is that they will help you, too.

Give your gripes to God. When David wrote Psalm 142, he was hiding in a dark, damp cave, fleeing from Saul and his bloodhounds. He was in deep soul trouble, burdened with complaints. David gives us a valuable lesson in how to pray when a complaining spirit quivers on the tip of our tongue.

> *I cry out to the LORD;*
> *I plead for the LORD's mercy.*
> *I pour out my complaints before him*
> *and tell him all my troubles.*

> *When I am overwhelmed,*
> *you alone know the way I should turn. (vv. 1–3 NLT)*

First, we see that David spilled it all out—not whispering but crying, begging, pouring out his gripes *to God alone*. Did you get that? He complained only to God.

Where do we go when we are irritated beyond belief with the man God gave us? Too often we play our complaints over and over in our mind until we feel crazy. Or tired of carrying them inside, we spill them out to a friend. While there are certainly times when we need to share our disappointments and frustrations with a trusted mentor, counselor, or close friend, they should not be where we go first. Yet that is not the case. I've been a woman for a lot of years, and in my experience, most of us go more quickly to a friend than to our Father.

David bundled up his gripes and took them to the only One who could bring relief. I love how C. H. Spurgeon says it: "We do not show our trouble to the Lord that He may see it, but that we may see Him. It is for our relief, and not for His information, that we make plain statements concerning our troubles. It does us much good to list our sorrows."[9]

Have you ever listed your complaints before the Lord? I have, and it helps. Find a place where you can be alone, take a pen and paper, and let your mind go wild. Record every complaint you have about your circumstances, about your husband. Don't skimp. Record it all, and then tear up your list. Fall on your face before God, and lay your complaints at His feet. David did this, and his griping turned to gratitude. Look at the next verses in Psalm 142:

Griping

> *I look for someone to come and help me,*
> *but no one gives me a passing thought!*

No one will help me;
　no one cares a bit what happens to me.
　(Ps. 142:4 NLT)

Gratitude

Then I pray to you, O LORD.
　I say, "You are my place of refuge.
　You are all I really want in life." (Ps. 142:5 NLT)

Pour out your complaints to God alone. This is the first thing you do. Next:

Accept your husband. If I asked you if you desired to bring praise to God with your choices and with your life as a wife, I think you'd answer, "Of course."

In Romans 15:5–7, we are specifically instructed in one way we can praise God:

> *May the God who gives endurance and encouragement give you a spirit of unity among yourselves as you follow Christ Jesus, so that with one heart and mouth you may glorify the God and Father of our Lord Jesus Christ.*
>
> 　*Accept one another, then, just as Christ accepted you, in order to bring praise to God. (NIV)*

God commands us—men, women, young and old, husbands and wives—to accept one another. He says that our acceptance of others produces a spirit of unity and brings glory to Him. What a great combination: praise and glory to God, and a spirit of unity. All as a result of our following God's command to accept one another.

Here's how I've personalized Romans 15:5–7 …

Linda: I can accept my husband because Christ first accepted me. I can extend to my man the same grace and understanding that Christ poured on me. Jesus forms the foundation of my acceptance and gives me the example to follow.

Now go back and read the above paragraph, putting *your* name in place of mine. Then, declare the following paragraph out loud to your Father God.

Christ accepted me unconditionally. Therefore, I can accept my husband, which promotes unity between us and brings praise and glory to God.

God makes it clear: Wives are to accept their husbands.

When a wife chooses not to accept her husband, she is sending him this message: "I don't like you as you are." A lack of acceptance will result in two things: (1) She will try to change her husband; (2) she will become a nag. Both have a devastating effect on the wife and on the marriage.

So ask God to help you accept your unique husband. When we have truly accepted our husbands, it makes this next step easier (notice, I did *not* say it was easy).

Move *from* Change HIM, Lord, *to* Change ME, Lord. Stormie Omartian in her excellent book *The Power of a Praying Wife* says God convicted her of heart issues and asked her to change her three-word favorite prayer, *Change HIM, Lord,* into God's favorite three-word prayer, *Change ME, Lord.*[10] I like Stormie. She is an honest woman. If we are as honest, we'll admit her favorite three-word prayer flows off our lips with greater ease than God's favorite three-word prayer.

One day I asked myself, *Why do you make continual suggestions to Jody, ask him continual questions, both of which Jody calls "sophisticated nagging"?* Taking a good, hard look within at my inner motives, I saw ugliness that was not pleasant to see: pride and selfishness lurked in my heart.

I am full of pride when I think my way of doing things is superior to my husband's way.

I am full of selfishness when I insist that he change and do things my way so that my life will be easier.

The Lord says to me as a wife, "Linda, why are you concentrating about the speck in Jody's eye, when you have a log in your eye? Get rid of the log in your own eye first" (my paraphrase of Matthew 7:3–5).

For most of my married life, I have used a simple chart to help get the log out of my eye. My natural response is to only see what Jody is doing wrong (somehow his weaknesses shout so much louder than mine!). I call this my Log Removal Chart. To help you grow toward accepting your husband, get out a sheet of paper or use a page on your computer. Make two columns. At the top of the left-hand column, write, *His Faults.* At the top of the right-hand column, write, *My Wrong Responses.* Your Log Removal Chart should look like this:

His Faults	My Wrong Responses

Now you get to fill it in!

Write down all your husband's faults. (This is the easy part.)

Go before the Lord and ask Him to reveal your wrong responses to your husband's faults. (This is the hard part.)

Will you be brave enough to pray God's favorite three-word prayer? *God, change me!*

One of the best things I did for my marriage was to ask God to change me; and to make a secret choice to accept Jody, who is so different from me; and to ask God to bring unity to our team and praise and glory to Him.

When I asked other wives to tell me about the best thing they did for their marriages, they said:

> *I placed my marriage in the Lord's hands and pray every day for it. Sometimes several times during the day. (Married twenty-four years)*

> *The best thing I did for my marriage was to quit pecking at my husband. I put these things in their proper place—in the quiet corner of my mind. Then I was able to see the good in this man I fell in love with. (Married fifteen years)*

> *My best thing was to be willing to change without my having to change him first. I made a choice to begin using more kind words, showing appreciation for things he did (even if not done my way), initiating sex, greeting him with a kiss every time we met (even if I was busy). Amazingly, in the last two years since my decision, my husband has changed to be more like the man I wanted. (Married fourteen years)*

> *I released my husband to a sovereign God who loves him more than I ever could. I have watched God build a godly man with gold, silver, and precious gems. I was trying to build a godly man out of LEGOs. (Married twenty-three years)*

I hope these comments convict and motivate you to put these ideas into practice. I can't promise that your husband will change if you do these things, but I can promise that *you* will change in a way that glorifies God and frees you from trying to take control of your husband.

I have one more idea to share with you. It is the topic of the next insight. Get ready for an amazing yet simple and practical project that I promise will push gripes out the door.

Insight 5: PUT ON A BRACELET

Will Bowen, a Lutheran pastor, wanted to help the people in his church improve their lives. He was convinced that thoughts held in mind produce after their kind. He knew that if we talk about what's wrong, it affects what we focus on, and we start seeing other things we don't like. Our negativity expands. His hope was to help the people in his church eradicate complaining from their lives, and, being a clever pastor, he devised a creative way to help them accomplish this.

He gave his church a 21-Day No-Complaint Challenge, complete with a purple bracelet that said A Complaint Free World.[11] He encouraged his congregation to put on the bracelet, and instructed them to move it from one wrist to the other every time a gripe escaped their lips. According to Pastor Bowen, wearing the bracelet makes you aware of when you complain, which can help you catch yourself before you do it the next time. The movement of switching the purple bracelet from wrist to wrist ingrains "Do not gripe!" in the brain.

When I read about the 21-Day No-Complaint Challenge, I told God I was willing to take the challenge and asked Him to help me become more aware of what tempts me to gripe and to help me stop my complaining.

Do you think you can live twenty-one days with no complaining, griping, murmuring, or nagging? If you think this is no big deal, let me give you the truth. The average person who takes the No-Complaint Challenge needs four to eight months to string together twenty-one gripe-free days. Are you surprised? Think it just can't be that hard? Pastor Bowen thought the same, but switching the bracelet from wrist to wrist convinced him that he complained all the time. A news reporter asked him how he was doing with this challenge. The pastor replied, "Well, after two weeks of really trying, I've made it almost six hours straight with no complaints."[12]

I put on the bracelet and watched and prayed, and within two hours, God showed me two things that bring out the whine in me. The first is technological gadgets. My iPhone, even my cute little pink notebook computer, drive me to gripe. This week while talking to a friend on my cell phone, voice messages started playing in the middle of the conversation. When I cut and pasted a paragraph in this manuscript, the text was also randomly pasted into an email. Jody, Mr. Computer Nerd, just shakes his head and says, "How do you do these things? They don't happen to anyone else."

The second thing that brings out griping is driving with Jody. My husband doesn't plan the best way to get someplace, and when he chooses the slowest route, my mouth opens automatically and says, "This way takes ten minutes longer." Wearing the bracelet has made me more aware of my critical, nagging attitude and is helping me to keep my mouth shut.

I challenged the women in my Bible study to put on a bracelet too. Read this comment from Sandy, a mom of four, during her first days of wearing the bracelet:

> *Well, the bracelet challenge is good. I'm discovering very specifi-cally when I complain—when I think Chad isn't doing his part to cooperate with my plans to deal with a situation, and when we're under pressure (i.e., getting to church on time, etc.). I'm making myself apologize to Chad each time I complain, just to drive it home. Getting tired of that already! I think I've had to apologize to him three times today!*

My funny friend Nanci sent me this email as she prepared for the bracelet challenge.

> *Before starting the No-Complaint Challenge, I wanted to under-stand exactly what I was to be sensitive to. Not that I had any lack of understanding about the word* complain, *but I wanted to be sure about* gripe. *I wondered, Is it* griping *to make a statement of fact, such as: Wow, it still smells like broccoli in this kitchen.*

I got up the next morning after reading the definition of gripe, walked into the kitchen, and said, "It stinks in here! I can't believe that broccoli smell is still here!" Now that falls under the definition of gripe: to complain naggingly or constantly grumble. It was the grumble that got me. Of course, I looked that up too. Grumble: to murmur or mutter in discontent. Yup, busted. I definitely grumbled/griped in the morning.

When I shared Nanci's email with the Bible study, everyone chuckled. But when I read what Valerie had written in her journal about what God had been showing her about griping, it brought all of us to a place of stunned silence.

Monday—I'm home from the hospital. I hugged my children and cried for joy to be in my home with those I love. I slept and rested. What a joy to be with Landon, to sit at the dinner table—even if I can't yet eat what they eat. I am in heaven on earth compared to my last three weeks....

Tuesday—Last night I slept in my own bed—what luxury! I was inches from Landon, and I had the privilege of listening to him breathe. It is a beautiful thing!

Thursday—Last night I slept five hours without waking. Hospital time is finally fading, and real time is coming back. It is wonderful! My wounds are healing, and I didn't have to come home with a wound vacuum. That was a huge blessing. My scars have multiplied, but so has my joy in the Lord. God is good. I have been living in heaven this past week. I have not changed my bracelet over once. Nothing like another prolonged stay in the hospital and a sixth major abdominal surgery in the last fifteen months to give

*me a large dose of perspective. I am here. I am alive. All is well
with my soul. Praise God!*

Do you remember me asking, "What will it take for us to make our marriage a priority, to concentrate on our blessings?" Valerie's spirit of gratitude caused each of us in the Bible study to be embarrassed at our complaints. Put on a bracelet and take the 21-Day No-Complaint Challenge. You will learn a lot about yourself. You can use any expandable bracelet or order your own "Gripes Be Gone" bracelets from www.LindaDillow.org.

If you had asked me four years ago, "Linda, do you gripe?" I would have said, "I've worked hard to train my mind to think before I speak, to stop words of griping." I think my husband and those who know me well would have said that I am not a complainer. Then my life was turned upside down, and I mean that literally. I fell down a staircase in an airport and landed on my head. Several hours later, I woke up in a trauma hospital and began the journey of healing from a traumatic brain injury. God is gracious; I can walk and talk and even speak at conferences, but I am not who I was before my accident. And one huge area of change is that my brain has forgotten all the years I worked with it to *not* let a complaining spirit be my spirit.

So, my friend, if you feel you're starting from ground zero, I'm right there with you. I'm having to relearn many things, especially "no griping." Jody would tell you that I almost daily ask him to forgive me for nagging, griping, sighing, complaining, and displaying an air of discontent with him. Today I feel like a first-class failure. I set aside the day to worship, wait, and write—a day of quiet with the Lord. But when Jody came home, thankfulness and praise to God was not what met him at the door. So I go back to God's Word, fall to my knees, and do what I've encouraged you to do:

First: I go to God alone and pour out my complaints.

Second: I make a secret choice to accept my husband.

Third: I move from, *Change HIM, Lord*, to *Change ME, Lord*.

Fourth: I wear my "Gripes Be Gone" bracelet.

I want to conquer griping for many reasons, but the most important is because of what the Lord says:

Linda,

In everything you do, stay away from complaining and arguing, so that no one can speak a word of blame against you. You are to live a clean, innocent life as a child of God in a dark world full of people who are crooked and stubborn. Shine out among them like a beacon light, holding out to them the Word of Life. (Phil. 2:14–16, author's paraphrase)

Have you ever seen a wife who overflows, not with gratitude but with griping? She is alive but her spirit is dead—years of grumbling, complaining, venting, griping, and nagging have killed the light in her eyes and the smile on her lips. The liar fed her lie upon lie about her husband, and she believed him. She grumbled and crumbled. The liar watches her and laughs, "A lighthouse? Ha! I won!"

I refuse to let the liar win.

I will trust in the One who gives me power through the Spirit.

I will retrain my brain to kick out gripes.

I will shine like a lighthouse on a fog-filled night to lead God's women away from griping to gratitude. Will you join me?

Dangerous Prayer!

Lord, I give You permission to search my heart and mind.
Please show me every day what it feels like to be my husband.

Am I Willing to Change My Attitude?

The man who has forgotten to be
thankful has fallen asleep in life.
Robert Louis Stevenson

The most important prayer in the world
is just two words long: Thank you.
Meister Eckhart

If you treat a man as he is, he will stay as he is. If you
treat him as if he were what he ought to be and could
be, he will become that bigger and better man.
Johann Wolfgang von Goethe

Thanksgiving is our dialect.
Ephesians 5:4 (MSG)

Insight 1: BUILDING A HOUSE OF GRATITUDE

Kaye turned on the car radio and heard Dr. Laura firmly tell a wife who had called in on her radio talk, "Stop whining! You have forgotten to be grateful." WHAMO! The exhortation hit home. Kaye says, "It was as though God took me by the shoulders and said, 'Hello! This is you, idiot!' Right at that moment in the car, I began to thank God for my husband and for every excellent quality he has."

Since then, Kaye says she has made a conscious effort to do the following:

- Every day she thanks God for her man, being sure to mention several specific qualities for which she is grateful.
- Every day she looks for ways to be a blessing to her husband (like trying to understand what pleases him, trying to anticipate his needs).
- She is committed to stay away from books, magazines, and TV shows that paint a false picture of what marriage and husbands ought to be like, and she makes an effort to be grateful for things as they are instead of trying to change the people around her.[1]

Kaye impresses me. What a woman! She heard truth—"You have forgotten to be grateful"—and immediately went into attack mode. She realized that griping was her native language and said, "I'm making a conscious choice to change me and learn to be thankful!"

Are you ready to do the same? I am!

Since I've put on the bracelet and taken the 21-Day No-Complaint Challenge, I've been more aware of the nagging, complaining, and murmuring words that come out of my mouth. It is not pleasant to see what fills my mind and mouth. I'm sure it hasn't been enjoyable for you to take this challenge either—but we had to see, to understand. Now it is time to replace the negative with the positive. Are you ready to replace the wrong with the right, to move gratitude into the house where griping has lived? God wants you to build a house of gratitude.

Did you know God says a wife is a builder? "A wise woman builds her home, but a foolish woman tears it down with her own hands" (Prov. 14:1 NLT).

I have thought a lot about how I build my marriage and how I tear it down. To me it has become fairly simple:

Griping tears down and destroys my sweetness with my husband.

Gratitude builds the sweetness in our relationship.

If you are wearing your "Gripes Be Gone" bracelet (and I hope, hope, hope you are), you are also becoming aware of whether you are demolishing or building your relationship with your husband. Are you building a house of gratitude? Is the word *gratitude* written on a plaque on your front porch? Each secret choice you make to have an attitude of gratitude is like an extra piece of wood that strengthens and reinforces your marriage house. You build either with quality materials and high craftsmanship or with just enough to get by. And you daily live with what your secret choices build.

Each time we say, "I will choose gratitude" or "I won't choose gratitude," we make a choice, a secret choice. I say "secret" because the choices that determine our faithfulness are made first on the inside, known only to us and God. Later, the results are seen by all.

Who watches, who observes what we build?

Single women watch. During the fourteen years my husband and I ministered in Communist Eastern Europe, we worked with many couples and a few singles. Something one of the single women said is engraved on my mind: "I've been watching the forty wives on our team and have decided that only two or three of them are really glad they are married." Only a few out of forty? This is sobering. I wonder what those watching me think. Do my words reflect delight in Jody or disapproval? Do my actions communicate that marriage is a wonderful union or an agonizing relationship to endure?

In her excellent book *Choosing Gratitude,* another godly single woman, Nancy Leigh DeMoss, says that many years ago she began giving a thirty-day encouragement challenge to wives: "I encouraged them to confront ingratitude and cultivate a thankful spirit in their marriage with two simple steps:

1. For the next thirty days, purpose not to say anything negative about your husband—not to him, and not to anyone else about him.

2. Every day for the next thirty days, express at least one thing you admire or appreciate about your husband. Say it to him and to someone else about him."[2]

Do you see what I see? Nancy didn't give this challenge to single women. She gave it to wives because she saw the same thing the single woman on our staff saw. My friend, single women are watching us.

Even more sobering, our children are watching. What would your son or daughter say about how you treat your husband? Would it be, "My mom loves being the wife of my dad," or "Mommy really doesn't like being married to Daddy." Women have told me, "My mother modeled a complaining spirit. I saw it every day." God forbid that when your daughter grows up, she says, "I learned to gripe from my mom."

I'm very aware that at least one more important Person is watching. My Father God is watching *me*. He is very serious about Linda embracing an attitude of gratitude. According to the commentaries, the word *thankful* is used over three hundred times in Scripture, but as I read my Bible I see thankfulness *everywhere*. Psalm 136 has twenty-six verses devoted solely to thanking God.

Here are a few of my favorite "thankful verses":

Praise the LORD!
  Oh give thanks to the LORD, for He is good;
  For His lovingkindness is everlasting. (Ps. 106:1)

I will give You thanks with all my heart. (Ps. 138:1)

Overflowing with gratitude. (Col. 2:7)

I want to overflow with thanksgiving. I want gratitude to pour out of my mind, my words, and my life! How grateful I am that God delights in turning my griping into gratitude. This paraphrase of Psalm 30:11–12 from *Psalms Now* by Leslie Brandt says it all:

> *And You turned my griping into gratitude,*
> *My screams of despair into proclamations of joy.*
> *Now I can explode with praises,*
> *And I will spend eternity in thanksgiving to You.*[3]

Oh, I long to live in a house of gratitude and explode with praises—to spend all eternity thanking God. I know God will do His part to turn my griping into gratitude, but it will also take work on my part. My problem is that griping is my mother tongue. Gratitude is my second language.

If you've ever tried to learn a second language, you know it takes practice. You must go over and over vocabulary words, repeating common phrases like a first grader. I remember my first project in German, the language I struggled to learn during our years in Europe. I picked up a chicken at the grocery store and was unpleasantly surprised to discover I'd purchased the *whole* bird—complete with head, dangling feet, and gooey innards. Chicken is sold this way in many parts of the world but not in the U.S., and I'd never had to prepare a whole chicken before. I learned what a ridiculously squeamish woman I was. The only way I could cut off that disgusting chicken head was to cover it with newspaper, close my eyes, and whack away! This experience motivated me to create my first German paragraph. With dictionary in hand, I wrote the following words, and then memorized them in preparation for my next chicken purchase.

So my German sounded something like this: *Ich möchte ein Huhn bitte. Können Sie bitte den Kopf und die Füsse abschneiden, die Innereien herausmachen und es in kleine Stücke schneiden?*

I was trying to express: "I would like a chicken. Would you please cut off the head and feet and clean out the insides? Then please cut it into small pieces."

The butcher laughed at my stumbling German, but he did what I asked.

How are you doing with the language of gratitude? Are you taking time to learn it? How does gratitude become a language we speak naturally?

First, remove the negative—thus the No-Complaint Bracelet project.

Second, impart the positive.

Earlier I shared with you that my brain injury somehow put griping back in me. Before my fall, thanking God and my husband came naturally to me. I had worked on having an attitude of gratitude. Then, overnight, it disappeared. So I went before my God and asked Him to show me how to relearn gratitude. I needed to find new ways to practice being thankful. Whether you need to relearn like me or are learning an attitude of gratitude for the first time, I believe my "growing in gratitude" projects will help you learn the language of gratitude. During the rest of this section, I'll outline some of these projects.…

Insight 2: GROWING IN GOD GRATITUDE

Last July I read Psalm 92:1–2 in my morning quiet time: "It is good to give thanks to the LORD and to sing praises to Your name, O Most High; to declare Your lovingkindness in the morning and Your faithfulness by night." I have read these verses many times before and always thought, *What a perfect thing to do; give thanks to God every morning for His lovingkindness and every night for His faithfulness.* That morning I decided to take the next four weeks to study these two words *faithfulness* and *lovingkindness* and to ask my Father to teach me how to thank Him. I wanted to be caught up in His lovingkindness before I leave my bed each morning and to delight in His faithfulness as I go to sleep each night.

For twenty-eight days I used Psalm 92:1–2 as my pattern of morning and evening worship to give thanks to God, and I recorded all I was learning in my journal. As I studied, I prayed, *My Lord, reveal, teach, and take me deeper in all You are as a God who loves me with lovingkindness. Take me deeper in all You are as a faithful God to me.*

What follows are my journal entries.

July 21

I learned today that the word "lovingkindness" is translated from the Hebrew word "hesed," which is used often in the Old Testament to signify God's covenant, steadfast love for me. In the Psalms (and this is true in Psalm 92) hesed is associated with the call to worship. I see that my morning and evening times of reflective thankfulness are all about worshipping the One who loves me, not just with a love like I love, but with a deep unfailing love.

Hesed is the unmerited and generous favor of God. Hesed love is gentle and always reaches out to the object of that love—which means me. Old Testament scholar Daniel Block describes hesed as "that quality that moves a person to act for the benefit of another without respect to the advantage that it might bring to the one who expresses it.... [T]his quality is expressed fundamentally in action rather than word or emotion."[4]

Father, thank You for leading me to learn about thanking You and Your precious lovingkindness to me. I see clearly that what I'm learning isn't just to encourage me; it's also meant to teach me how to love my husband. I'm to do things that are best for Jody—not for me. To love him with my actions, not just my words.

July 30

I love it, my Father, that not one English word can hold all the meaning of hesed, so we string words together. It is never just love but "steadfast, covenant-love," "unfailing love," and "lovingkindness." It is like when I talk to one of our grandchildren. Just saying "I love you" isn't enough, so it is, "I love you more than all the ice cream in the whole world!" Thank You that You needed more than one word to express Your everlasting love for me ... that touches me in a deep place.

August 4

Time to move on from lovingkindness to faithfulness. In Psalm 92, the Hebrew word for faithfulness is "aman," or its derivative "emunah." These two words carry the ideas of firmness, steadiness, sureness, steadfastness, faithfulness, trust, honesty, safety, and certainty. When faithfulness is applied to God, it is talking about His believability. Beth Moore says, "Faithfulness is resting in His certainty, being persuaded by His honesty, trusting in His reality, being won over by His veracity.... [B]eing sure that He's sure and believing He's worth believing."[5]

So when I meditate on God's faithfulness in the evening, I am thanking Him that He is always true and always the same, that He is good, even when I can't understand Him, and that He loves me, even when I don't feel His love. Beth Moore says that the degree of our faithfulness to others is the direct result of our regard for God's faithfulness to us.[6] That is some statement, and in my spirit, I know it is true.

August 9

Lord, it just hit me that love and faithfulness are fruit of the Spirit. They are what I need to love this complicated man You gave me. My personal Marriage Purpose Statement is the word faithful, and forever faithful is what I long to be. So thank You, my Father, for leading me to thank You for just what I need. I see that my faithfulness and love is the direct result of how big and wide and deep Your love and faithfulness is to me. Teach me, please.

August 15

Oh, I am excited about what I learned today! Psalm 59:10 says that God in His lovingkindness will meet me. I see my Father coming to sit with me and share a cup of tea. How precious that He meets me in His lovingkindness. I feel embraced by His love. I've been walking around all day thanking the Holy One for personally meeting with me in His unfailing love.

August 21

Lord, I thank You today for showing me in Psalm 36 that Your lovingkindness is as vast as the heavens and that Your faithfulness reaches beyond the clouds. As I sit by this beautiful lake, drinking in your serene presence, I thank You that You declare that Your lovingkindness is precious (Ps. 36:7) and that You pour out Your lovingkindness on those who love You (Ps. 36:10). Because You declare this to me today, I proclaim the preciousness of Your unfailing love to me. Thank You for this quiet day to bask in Your presence and literally feel the delight of Your lovingkindness poured out on me. Oh, how I love You!

Six months have passed, and I am still thanking God and praising Him every morning for His lovingkindness and every evening for His faithfulness. I have felt my gratitude growing. I've been focusing on God gratitude, but it is overflowing and turning into gratitude for my husband.

How about you? It is really very simple to imitate my God-Gratitude Project. Why don't you get out your Bible and memorize Psalm 92:1–2? It is easy to remember—even my injured brain learned it quickly. Then begin to journal and see your gratitude grow!

Insight 3: GROWING IN HUSBAND GRATITUDE

I've been asking myself more hard questions: How often do I take Jody for granted? Do I let him know how much his encouragement means to me? Do I thank him for little things, like filling my car with gas? Or do I assume he knows I appreciate that he does these things, and so say nothing?

My wise editor and friend, Liz, told me that her husband, Casey, wakes up every day and asks, "How can I make Liz happy today?" When she told me this, I said, "Wow! That's amazing." I asked Liz if she knew how rare her husband is. "Yeah, I know," Liz replied. "I'm so blessed, and I know it is easy to take my great husband for granted."

When my heart is full of gratitude, it encourages me not to take Jody for granted. My Psalm 92 Project took me deeper in God gratitude, so I asked my Lord to show me how to go deeper in husband gratitude. He encouraged me to do two things:

1. Begin a Thankful Journal. Bridal showers are filled with an atmosphere of anticipation. I was invited to a shower for the daughter of a dear friend, and my gift bag was filled with practical encouragements for her first year of marriage. One gift captured the interest of the bride-to-be—a Thankful Journal. It was a simple journal labeled, "Kelly's Thankful Journal." These instructions were included:

> 1. Choose one day each week to be your time to write in this journal—Sunday is a good time.
>
> 2. Reflect over the last week with your new husband and record your "I am thankful" for James because_____, or I am thankful for our marriage because _____.
>
> 3. Write a prayer of thanks to God.

If Kelly writes in her Thankful Journal for fifty-two weeks, even if she records her gratitude for only twenty-five weeks of her first year of marriage, think what a treasure she will have! How I wish someone had given me a Thankful Journal and encouraged me to write my thank-yous about my new husband when Jody and I married in 1964. How special it would be to be able to read the thoughts, thank-yous, and prayers I wrote when I was a twenty-one-year-old bride!

Whether you are newly married, an older married woman like me, or somewhere in between, I encourage you to keep a Thankful Journal this year. This project isn't just for the first year of marriage; it's a good idea for every year.

I've written thank-yous to God in journals over the years, but now I have a special journal just for gratitude. I have been writing in it for three months now. Today has not been a good marriage day. When I was on my knees in prayer, the Lord whispered to me to get out my Thankful Journal and read it. Guess what happened in my heart? As I read twelve weeks of gratitude, I remembered how much I have to be grateful for. I even remembered why I love this man!

My second project took me still deeper in husband gratitude.

2. Dwell on the positive. You have probably read Philippians 4:8 several times, or even memorized it, but have you ever directly applied it to your husband?

> *Finally, brethren, whatever is true, whatever is honorable, whatever is right, whatever is pure, whatever is lovely, whatever is of good repute, if there is any excellence and if anything worthy of praise, dwell on these things.*

I began my project by looking through many translations of this verse and making my own paraphrase.

> *Linda, fix your thoughts on what is true and worthy of respect. Dwell on what is right and pure and lovely about Jody. Think about things that are excellent and worthy of praise in this man you married.*

Next, I made a list of these words:

- True

- Worthy of respect
- Right
- Pure
- Lovely
- Excellent
- Worthy of praise

Each day of the week, I thought about one of the above attributes and asked God to reveal how Jody displayed that quality, and then I wrote it all in my Thankful Journal. For example:

Sunday—True

Jody is committed to truth, and he lives what is true. This man doesn't lie. I can trust him.

Monday—Worthy of Respect

Jody has saved for our retirement, even when, in our thirties, I argued with him about it and said, "We don't have the money for this." He has started a college fund for each of our grandchildren. Few husbands and fathers have done what Jody has done. As I write this, I hear God whisper: Linda, have you told Jody how you respect him for his financial faithfulness?

Tuesday—Just

Jody fights for what is right and just. Whether it is evolution and creation or a political issue, he is on the side of right (or what he is convinced is right).

I did this exercise for several weeks and was amazed that God brought different things to my mind each time. Every week I thanked Jody for who he is and for all the positive attributes I see in him.

Maybe you're thinking, *If I did this project, all I would think of is negative qualities.* Go back to Philippians 4:8 and read it again. It doesn't say, "If *everything* is excellent and worthy of praise"; it says, "If there is anything excellent and worthy of praise." If you commit to dwelling on the positive, I believe God will show you something excellent in your husband's character, something worthy of praise.

Don't delay! Today is the day to express your thanks to your husband. My friend Peggy is so grateful she didn't delay.

> *Life can be so busy that we forget to be thankful. I am so thankful for the years of loving Don. Now I watch as the brain tumors slowly take him away from me. I knew this would be our last Valentine's Day, and I wanted it to be special. Unexpectedly, I found three love letters I'd written to Don over the years. I decided sharing them with him would be the best Valentine's card I could give him.*

> *1985: Thank you for loving me for twenty-nine years. I still get excited just to be with you and hold your hand.*

> *1988: After thirty-two years, I am overwhelmed at the privilege of being your wife.*

> *1995: Thank you for loving me unconditionally and unselfishly and continually looking for ways to make me happy. Thank you for giving me the freedom to develop my gifts. I am so grateful for you!*

> *2010. Three months after I gave Don his special Valentine, he went to be with the Lord. I am alone. I'm so thankful I expressed my gratitude to him.*

Don't delay! Tell your husband you are thankful for him today!

Let's not wait until something happens that pushes us to think about our blessings. May we work to grow deeper in husband gratitude *now*. May we grow deeper in husband gratitude, may we open our mouths and express the positive we see in our husband, not only to him, but to others.

Practical Gratitude

Here are some additional Gratitude Projects from women in my survey:

Every night before my husband and I go to sleep we say our "I appreciates." We take the time to mention three things we appreciated about each other that day. They have to be different every day—and it is a wonderful time of connection and communication. (Married three years)

I have just begun to reach out to my husband with thanksgiving. It was harder at first, but now I find the words rolling off my lips. I now thank him for all of his many acts of kindness towards me. This simple act pleases him so much. (Married forty years)

I made a decision to do at least one kind act every day for my husband. (Married thirteen years)

Every night I write down five things that I am thankful for about my husband. I write about big things, little things, good things. First thing in the morning, I read what I wrote the night before and start my day with positive thoughts about my husband. (Married seventeen years)

Insight 4: OFFER A SACRIFICE OF THANKSGIVING

It's not hard to thank God when my husband is loving me sweetly and tenderly. I feel thankful. But thanking God when my husband is not loving me sweetly and tenderly? That is beyond hard. I definitely do not feel thankful. Instead, I must choose in my will to be thankful.

God rejoices when a wife makes that hard choice to give thanks (1 Thess. 5:18). Women have asked me, "Linda, isn't it fake to give thanks when you really want to punch your husband?" Good question. Dr. John Mitchell, cofounder of Multnomah University, answers it like this: "To give thanks when you don't feel like it is not hypocrisy; it's obedience."[7]

If you struggle with how to give thanks when you don't feel like it, I encourage you to read through psalms. You don't need to stuff your negative feelings or sweep them under an imaginary carpet. David poured out his heart to God (Ps. 62:8). If I say it like I see it, he sometimes spewed his questions, his grief and pain, all over His God. God was big enough to take David's doubts and questions and to bring him to a place of laying it all down as a sacrifice to the One he loved. God says He receives our anguished thanks as a sacrificial offering.

> *"He who offers a sacrifice of thanksgiving honors Me." (Ps. 50:23)*

> *Through Him then, let us continually offer up a sacrifice of praise to God, that is, the fruit of lips that give thanks to His name. (Heb. 13:15)*

Three words jump out at me from Hebrews 13:15 about a sacrifice of thanksgiving:

1. Continually. I am to offer God a sacrifice of praise over and over, whether I feel like it or not.
2. Sacrifice. My sacrifice of praise will burn; it will hurt.
3. Thanks. I am to give thanks to God over and over for things that hurt and are anything but good.

As I write this, I have an opportunity to offer a sacrifice of thanksgiving. I do not feel thankful that my house is a construction zone due to the water damage to all three floors. I do not feel thankful for the grimy dust everywhere. I do not feel thankful that the toilet is sitting in my wonderful big bathtub. My nightly bath is sacred to me. Nor do I feel thankful for the continual pounding and drilling. I want quiet, peace, and order. Instead, I have noise, confusion, and chaos. It is time to offer a sacrifice of thanksgiving.

So I go to the Lord and pray: *Lord, I don't understand Your timing, but I say, "My times are in Your hand" (Ps. 31:15). You know this book is due to my editor in twelve days. You know chaos is hard for my brain. You know everything. I don't feel thankful, but I choose in my will to offer a sacrifice of thanksgiving to You. I thank You that You are going to work everything together for good, even though I don't understand Your ways.*

In Hebrews 13:5, thanksgiving and praise are linked together as a sacrifice. I love what Merlin Carothers says:

> *I have come to believe that the prayer of praise is the highest form of communion with God, and one that always releases a great deal of power into our lives. Praising Him is not something we do because we feel good; rather it is an act of obedience. Often the prayer of praise is done in sheer teeth-gritting willpower; yet when we persist in it, somehow the power of God is released into us and into the situation.*[8]

I experienced God's power to bring peace in the midst of my house disaster, which is really a little thing. But God can—and does—release His power in us, even in horrific situations. I witnessed this power being released in Emma. Here is what she wrote in her journal one morning:

> *I don't know what I thought pornography would be like, but when I clicked on that site he left on the browser and saw what he had been looking at, it devastated my heart beyond words. Is*

this what he wants from me? Is this what he thinks I am? Is this who he is?

He betrayed our intimacy—there's nothing deeper to betray. And he did it when I was giving him myself with more and more abandon. I feel so inadequate—all of me isn't good enough for him. I feel so devalued—some naked woman doing vile things on a computer screen matters more than everything I am and everything we are together. How do I give myself to him again?

Lord, I have nowhere to go but to You. I have no answers, no ideas, no solutions. You say: "Offer to God a sacrifice of thanksgiving … Call upon Me in the day of trouble; I shall rescue you, and you will honor Me" (Ps. 50:14–15).

This is my day of trouble, Lord. I thank You because You will rescue me and I will honor You. Lord, thank You that through-out Your Word You show me You want to exchange all that You are for all of me—to exchange your liberty for my captivity, Your comfort for my grief, Your beauty for my ashes, Your oil of gladness for my mourning, Your mantle of praise for my spirit of fainting. You offer Your light for my darkness, Your strength for my weakness, Your hand for my stumbling, Your joy for my sorrow, Your truth for my chains, Your nearness for my broken heart.

You are my rock, my fortress, and my deliverer. Thank You that I can cling to You. Thank You that You are complete, never lacking, faithful, and secure. You are my beloved. I wait for You. I rest in You.

How could Emma choose an attitude of thankfulness in the aftermath of her husband's betrayal? If you have ever discovered your husband looking at pornography, you likely wanted to scream, kick (preferably him), run away, or just sit down and weep forever. You were filled with anger at your husband, and maybe even at God for not intervening and keeping this from happening. I'm sure Emma felt some of these things. I know, too, what she wrote for her Marriage Purpose Statement, and I share it with you here because it will help you see the deep commitment behind her sacrifice of thanksgiving.

Emma used the beautiful love passage in 1 Corinthians 13 as the basis for her Marriage Purpose Statement:

Lord, through Your love in me, I choose …

To love Sam patiently, with a willingness to suffer long— when he doesn't understand, when I don't understand, and when neither of us does; when we face long-term struggles, battle sin, and when our weaknesses collide.

To love Sam in kindness, when I'm angry, hurt, tired, and even premenstrual.

To love Sam without jealousy—toward his role, his privileges, or toward other women for what they have in marriage. I will choose thankfulness for who he is and what we are together.

To love Sam without bragging about what I know or think I know, but by choosing instead to build him up.

To love Sam without pride and arrogance … when I'm wrong and when I'm right or when I think I'm right. I choose to have a humble heart that views him as more important than myself.

To love Sam without being rude and critical when I see his weaknesses, when I'm hurt, angry, or frustrated. I choose to have a gentle and quiet spirit.

To love Sam without being self-seeking when I feel like my rights and feelings aren't seen or respected. I choose to have Your attitude, Jesus, to lay down every right I have and entrust myself and my needs to You.

To love Sam without being easily provoked when my feelings are hurt or his actions unjust. I choose to be quick to listen, slow to speak, and slow to become angry.

To love Sam without keeping a record of what he's done wrong. I choose to forgive unconditionally and continually, not holding wrongs I've suffered against him.

To love Sam by never delighting in evil … in our marriage or in either of us personally. I will rejoice when truth wins out.

To love Sam by having an attitude in our marriage that bears all things, believes all things, hopes all things, and endures all things.

Oh, Lord, give me Your love for Sam that will never fail.

Emma and her husband are doing well together. God used her sacrifice of thanksgiving to humble Sam, and he sought help for his addiction. He is accountable to a Christian counselor and is moving forward on the path to freedom.

God asks each of us to offer a sacrifice of thanksgiving. Sometimes our sacrificial offer is for a house in chaos, or for a brain injury, or for a marriage conflict. And like Emma, sometimes we offer to God a sacrifice of thanksgiving for very difficult things. I know that in the offering, God breathes into us power and peace, as He did for Emma. He is so pleased when we offer this deepest form of gratitude, a sacrifice of thanksgiving.

Insight 5: A DANGEROUS PRAYER

When Lynne was praying fervently for a friend's husband, God gave her the conviction that she was to pray for her own husband with the same passion and fervor. So Lynne prayed a dangerous prayer: *Lord, show me how to be devoted in prayer to my husband.* I'll let her tell you what happened next.

> *I prayed about the pain David was struggling through and asked God to intervene with power in his life. Then I called and told him what I saw in him, how God had gifted him and called him to leadership. I told him that I believed in him and that I was committed to pray for him.*
>
> *It was amazing to see his response—it had been a long time since I had breathed life into him with my words. We were both humbled by this experience. It was an unspoken softness we had for one another. I was humbled that I could pray so fervently for my friend's husband, who was missing, but miss my own husband simply by not praying for him.*

Many of us want to be devoted to prayer, but our requests are usually for a friend in need, someone in our church who has cancer, or the orphans with AIDS in Africa. Is it easier to pray for others than it is to pray for my husband? I think it is.

I know the book of Colossians has thankfulness flowing off of its pages, that each of its four chapters speaks of thankfulness. Since I am on a mission to grow in gratitude, I decided to get my Bible and study all Paul had to say. I discovered that, yes, gratitude is a major theme found in each chapter of Colossians (1:3, 12; 2:6–7; 3:15–17; 4:2). As I read through this precious love letter from God, I sensed He wanted me to paraphrase what it says to me about being a wife and then apply the message to my attitude toward my husband. Here is what I wrote:

> *As a wife, I give thanks to God the Father of our Lord Jesus Christ—praying always for you, my husband (Col. 1:3).*

As a wife, I am always thanking the Father, who lets Jody and me walk in His light together (Col. 1:12).

As a wife, I am to walk by faith and build my life on Christ, and I am to overflow with gratitude for Jody (Col. 2:6–7).

As a wife, I am to be filled with God's peace. I am called to live in peace with Jody. AND always be thankful (Col. 3:15).

As a wife, I am to sing psalms and hymns and spiritual songs to God with a thankful heart (Col. 3:16).

As a wife, whatever I do, whatever I say, is to be as Jesus' representative, giving thanks through Him to God the Father (Col. 3:17).

As a wife, I am to devote myself to prayer for Jody with an alert mind and thankful heart (Col. 4:2).

Lots to think about, but the verse that pierced my heart is the last one. I am to devote myself to prayer for my husband. How am I to do this? With an alert mind and a thankful heart. It is the word *devote* that reaches deep into my spirit. *Devote* is such a strong word, implying a heavy commitment. What am I really devoted to? The dictionary says that "to devote" is to give of oneself, one's time, energy. God is asking me to sacrifice my time and my energy to pray for Jody. Only God will know if I make this deep secret choice.

When I sacrifice in this way, I'm not just to pray whatever comes to my mind, I am to be *alert* in my mind—attuned to Jody, attuned to his joys, attuned to his sorrows, attuned to his frustrations. I am to be *alert* to how I can help him, to how I can encourage him. Being alert is the opposite of being uninterested or passive. God is asking me to be keyed in to where Jody is physically, emotionally, and spiritually.

How easy it is to live in the same house, sleep in the same bed, and be oblivious to who our husband is at this moment and to who he is becoming! When we devote ourselves to pray for him, it is a sacrifice of time, of love, and of devotion. But when we devote ourselves to praying for him *with an alert mind and thankful heart,* we've given our husband the greatest gift we can give him.

My friend, I hope you can feel yourself growing in gratitude. *Remember, reflect,* and *respond.* Open your mouth and express your thankfulness to God and to your husband. While you are at it, throw some thanks your children's way; they need it too! God is in the business of changing you! He is about changing your native language from griping to gratitude!

Dangerous Prayer!

Lord, please teach me to speak the language of gratitude.

What Will It Take for Me to Get Close to You?

Insight 1: SURPRISE! MEN AND WOMEN ARE DIFFERENT

One of the most beautiful descriptions of emotional intimacy I've ever read was written by my friend Nanci. She and her husband waded through rough waters in their marriage and came out swimming strong on the other side. Here is what she says about emotional intimacy:

> *Emotional intimacy is being "naked and unashamed." To be fully known; my darkest thoughts, hateful words, biggest disappointments, and greatest fears—and yet be fully loved and accepted. To*

know that I have given my heart to my husband, that he takes seriously the role of protector; that he is careful with my heart. And I am careful with his heart. It is knowing him so well and having such a deep understanding of him that I can trust him beyond circumstances. It is being so entwined with one another, yet so different, that we are like one plant putting off two very different blooms.

Marriage is the adventure of discovering one another so you might deeply share:

A soul intimacy

A body intimacy

A spirit intimacy

The three intimacies together are what yield oneness. Sex without soul intimacy is empty, satisfying only the body. Soul and body intimacy without spirit oneness is missing God's best. God made us three-dimensional people. Husband and wife are to meet body, soul, and spirit; the result will be a lover-best friend relationship.

God agrees.

Yet, many wives wonder, *Is it really possible to have emotional intimacy with my husband? We are just so different! Can I get close to him, and what will it take?*

I can only share with you how one right-brained-engineer-type man (Jody) and one left-brained-relational-type woman (me) created deep emotional oneness in our marriage. And in truth I can only share my part, because I can only make choices for me. What did I do to move closer to Jody?

The answer to that question starts on the first page of this book, because everything I've been writing about has been part of the process. I asked myself, *Who or what is really important to me? Is Jody first in my heart, or are the kids first?* I asked God to show me what it felt like to be my husband. When I saw that my pride and selfishness were sending Jody the message that "My way of living life is better than yours," and when I realized how I'm more prone to gripe and complain than to express gratitude, I asked God to change me. Truly, growing in gratitude transformed how I see my husband. When a wife asks these hard questions about herself, it sets the stage for emotional intimacy with her husband. Intimacy means "into me see." I can't see into Jody's heart if I'm fighting against our differentness or trying to change him.

That is the background. Jody's and my emotional intimacy didn't happen overnight. It happened over the many years of our marriage.

Moving closer to Jody also involved acknowledging that he is another species. This fact is often the subject of jokes like this humorous blurb I found on the Internet:

How to Treat a Woman

Wine her. Dine her. Call her. Hold her. Surprise her.
Compliment her. Smile at her. Listen to her. Laugh with her.
Cry with her. Romance her. Encourage her. Believe in her.
Pray with her. Pray for her. Cuddle with her. Shop with her.
Give her jewelry. Buy her flowers. Hold her hand.
Write love letters to her. Go to the ends of the earth and back
again for her.

How to Treat a Man

Show up naked. Bring chicken wings. Don't block the TV.[1]

Indeed, men and women are different. It's one thing to read about these differences; it's something else altogether to live with such a foreign creature. That is no laughing matter! I realized that if I wanted emotional closeness with Jody, *I needed to stop fighting our differences and try to understand what makes him feel close to me.*

I'm going to tell you a closely kept secret about men. Men don't talk about it, so your husband may not even be aware of it. Closeness comes for him when you are body to body or shoulder to shoulder. Jody feels emotional intimacy with me in sexual intimacy. One husband said this about the connectedness he felt after making love with his wife: "I feel whole and complete. My life is at peace. I thank God for you and the special gift it is to love and be loved by you." Sounds like emotional intimacy to me! Another man said that after loving his wife sexually, he can go outside and smell the flowers. He can walk with his wife and have deep communication. *Sexual intimacy opens him to emotional connection.* Write that one down; it is important that you get this in your brain.

When women want to feel emotionally connected, they talk. Words are spoken, hearts connected, and secrets shared. Men, very different from us, can feel close without having any eye connection or heart contact. No secrets shared, very few words spoken. Being shoulder to shoulder is enough. Shoulder-to-shoulder connection is what happens when men watch football, basketball, or any kind of ball together. They eat yummy things and make comments about their favorite team. Their eyes are on the screen, not on each other. But in their male brains and hearts, they are connecting.

It took me a long time to understand this, and to act on my understanding. Jody feels close to me when we go to the Santa Fe Trail together. He takes off and runs four miles. I walk two miles listening to worship music and have a sweet time of prayer while waiting for him to finish his jog. We get back in the car, share about our respective exercise times, and drive home. To me, we are two people doing two different things. Jody loves it. I entered into his life and did an "activity" with him.

Jody studied engineering. His brain is analytical, focused—very unlike mine. I smile inside when I look back over the years and realize how this left-brained man of mine has learned to enter deeply into emotional intimacy with me.

Last month he took me out to dinner for my birthday and then said he had a surprise for me. This man who doesn't do details took me to our camper, where he had spent hours preparing it for my birthday. All of the little things he did spoke love to me. The cake even said, "I love Linda." (I asked him if the woman at the bakery laughed when he told her what to write. She did.) I had asked Jody that week what emotional intimacy meant to him. On a beautiful flowery card, Jody had written …

> *Emotional intimacy is sharing dreams and desires, plans and adventure. It is both encouragement and comfort. It is being best friends and lovers. Your love has made this real in my life.*

Not bad for a left-brained male.

It *is* possible for a husband and wife, two very different species who view life through different lens, to develop a lover/best-friend intimacy. Jody and I are proof that it can happen.

Insight 2: WE BOTH HAVE GAPS

If you haven't seen the original *Rocky*, rent it! The film is worth the rental price just to observe the love relationship between Rocky and Adrian. The big hunk and the wallflower from the pet shop were definitely an unexpected match. Adrian's brother, Paulie, an insensitive goon, could not figure out why Rocky would be attracted to his sister.

"What's the attraction?" Paulie asked.

"I don't know—she fills gaps."

"What's 'gaps'?"

"I don't know, she's got gaps, I got gaps, together we fill gaps."

In a simple but profound way, Rocky hit upon a truth. He was saying that without him, Adrian had empty places in her life, and without her, he had empty places in his. But when the two of them got together, they helped fill the gaps; they met the needs in the other.

God agrees with Rocky: All men and women have gaps. In Genesis 2, He clearly defines the deep-felt need of both man and woman—the need for an intimate companion.

In the garden of Eden, Adam had a perfect relationship with God, a perfect environment, something to occupy his time, and an infinity of things to explore. But he also had a gap. One thing was missing from his life: someone to walk through the garden with, to work with, to laugh with, to share with; someone to love. Adam had everything, but Adam was alone. Adam had gaps.

In the Chinese language, entire words are written with one symbol. Often two completely unlike symbols, when put together, have a meaning different from their two separate components. A beautiful example is the symbol of man and that of woman. When these symbols are combined, man plus woman equals good, and that is exactly what God said. In the creation account, we read seven times that "God saw that it was good." Then in Genesis 2:18, God says something is "not good"—"Then the LORD God said, 'It is not good for the man to be alone; I will make him a helper suitable for him.'"

When God brought the woman to Adam, his response was beyond good—he was ecstatic: "This is it!" (Gen. 2:23 TLB). Today he might say, "YES!" or "Wow, right on! She's the one!" Adam was definitely pleased with his "suitable helper." God had created for him a companion, someone to share the challenges of life with. Someone who would feel as he felt, exude joy at discovery, and problem solve with him in times of puzzlement. A companion who would discover what intimacy looked like with him. A wife to fill his gaps.

What an indescribably beautiful provision by God! Our needs for an intimate companion perfectly met in marriage. C. S. Lewis was an older bachelor when he married his beloved wife, Joy. In his powerful way with words, he describes their deep emotional intimacy:

[We] feasted on love, every mode of it—solemn and merry, romantic and realistic, sometimes as dramatic as a thunderstorm,

sometimes comfortable and unemphatic as putting on your soft slippers.... She was ... my pupil and my teacher, my subject and my sovereign; and always, holding all these in solution, my trusty comrade, friend, shipmate, fellow-soldier. My mistress, but at the same time all that any man friend ... has ever been to me.[2]

C. S. Lewis discovered God's answer to man's gap was to give him a wife, someone who would come alongside him and be a vital part of his finding fulfillment.

Both husbands and wives carry within the need for an intimate companion. Both also have a driving need that is gender specific.

For the wife, her greatest need is for security. For the husband, his greatest need is for significance.

In a beautiful way, God set about filling the gaps of both husband and wife (Eph. 5:25–33). His command to the husband would fill the wife's *love gap*. His command to the wife would fill the husband's *respect gap*. God commanded:

The husband: Love your wife sacrificially (Eph. 5:25, 28).

The wife: Respect your husband unconditionally (Eph. 5:33).

I've gone on a hunt, searched this passage for an *if* that wrapped God's commands with conditions. It would read like this:

IF your husband is tender, understanding, compassionate, IF he loves you sacrificially every day, every hour, in every situation, THEN you respect him.

I can't find an *if* in this passage, and believe me, I've looked hard. It makes more sense to me to have conditions. *If* a wife is an evil shrew, why should a husband sacrifice to love her? *If* a husband is a slovenly couch potato, why should a wife respect him unconditionally? Get out your Bible and read Ephesians 5:21–33 carefully. Did you find an *if?* Nope. I didn't either. God clearly sums it all up to both partners; He believes this is so important that He repeats His commands again:

> *So again I say, each man must love his wife as he loves himself,*
> *and the wife must respect her husband. (Eph. 5:33 NLT)*

Did you notice the *must?*

An *if* means there are conditions. A *must* means no conditions. A *must* says, JUST DO IT.

In his excellent book *Love and Respect,* Dr. Emerson Eggerichs sums it up this way:

> *A wife has one driving need—to feel loved. When that need is met,*
> *she is happy. A husband has one driving need—to feel respected.*
> *When that need is met, he is happy.*[3]

May it be so in your marriage.

Your part in creating emotional intimacy with your husband not only involves admitting that you and your husband both have gaps. We'll talk more about how you can fill your husband's gaps, but first I want to talk with you about your divine calling as a wife.

Insight 3: A WIFE'S DIVINE CALLING

God has given each wife a divine calling. We need to go back to Genesis to see this call.

> *Then the LORD God said, "It is not good for the man to be alone;*
> *I will make him a helper suitable for him." (Gen. 2:18)*

Man's "suitable helper"[4] would provide the missing pieces from the puzzle of his life. She would complete him as a qualified, corresponding partner. This is good, but there is more: A mystery surrounds this one called helper. As the Creator declared His chosen name for her, I suspect the angels looked on in unbelief and exclaimed something like this: "This is unheard of! How can this be? She is set apart as special. The almighty God, Creator of heaven and earth honors her—He actually gives her one of His holy names! Oh, she is so blessed!"

Why were the angels so excited? What is this special name of God's that He shares with wives—with you? In Hebrew it is the name *Ezer*. In English it is translated as *helper*.

Helper? You may have mixed feelings about that name. It sounds drab, dreary, and depressing. Webster even defines a helper as "one that helps; especially a relatively unskilled worker who assists a skilled worker, usually by manual labor."[5] Sounds like a *hausfrau* from the 1940s, clothed in a housedress with a cutesy apron, down on her knees scrubbing a floor, right? But this is *not* what God has in mind here. Put those images—which are incorrect—aside and try to get your mind and heart around God's meaning of His name *Ezer*.

Ezer is used twenty-one times in the Old Testament and almost always refers to God. It is His name. The Lord God Almighty is called our helper:

> *"My father's God was my helper." (Ex. 18:4 NIV)*

> *You [God] are the helper of the fatherless. (Ps. 10:14 NIV)*

> *The LORD is with me; he is my helper. (Ps. 118:7 NIV)*

> *Our soul waits for the LORD;*
> *He is our help and our shield. (Ps. 33:20)*

Then in Genesis 2:18–25, God takes this strong name *Ezer* and in effect says, "Now you, the one called wife, have the same privilege and the responsibility that I have. I give you one of My names, Helper. Being a helper is godlike. As I come alongside you as your Helper, I ask you to come alongside your husband, and fill his respect gap as his personal, private, intimate helper. *Only you* will know what respect looks like for him. *Only you* can become his intimate ally, his closest companion. *Only you* will know how to design a personal program of helping for your unique man."

I am not talking about being your husband's secretary, seamstress, gardener, or accountant. As wives we are to help our husbands; it is part of the essence of who we are as women. It is within the fabric of our created being. However, the specific expression of what we do as a result of being helpers is unique for each marriage relationship. And it will vary over the course of our lifetimes.

While writing this chapter, I went to Jody and asked, "What practically can I do in this season of life to be a help to you?" His answer surprised me: "Come with me when I travel and speak." Groan. I already travel and don't want to travel more. But I had asked and told God, "I'll do what he suggests." So the next time Jody got ready to leave for a trip, I had my plane ticket in hand. However, I never got on the plane. The water damage to our house happened just at that time, and I needed to stay to talk to the insurance adjuster and supervise various workmen. But I tried, and my attitude of wanting to be there spoke love to my husband and blessed him. Next time, I might even make it on the plane.

My friend Tamra has thought deeply about being a helper to her husband, Barry, as is illustrated in her Marriage Purpose Statement, which I want to share with you:

> *Father, I thank You for forgiving me for all the years my marriage*
> *was dominated by my self-centeredness. I tossed Barry a bone of*
> *submission on the big decisions regarding career, church home,*

moving, etc., but in my daily life I was so much more contentious than gracious, so much more competing than completing, thinking so much more about my own interests rather than his. I was friendly to everyone else, but then I came home and was too often a grump.

Lord, I thank You for opening my eyes twelve years ago to see that Barry was not created for me, but I for him. That is part of the essence of who You have made me: I am to complement Barry in his person and in his work. Father, I pray that You would continue to reveal what that looks like in our marriage. I ask that I would have eyes to see and the wisdom to know how I can be a true helper and complement to this man to whom I have the privilege of being married. I pray that I will bring him good and not harm all the days of my life. I pray I will walk worthy of his heart safely trusting in me. I pray that all You have put within me will first serve my husband's abilities and life calling. I pray we will fulfill all of the will of God in our lifetime as we do the same work together, or complementary work that is different, and that all of our efforts will be in harmony toward the same goal.

Thank You, Father! I have had the joy and privilege of getting to know my husband more in the last twelve years than I did in the first fourteen. I was so blinded by my own ambitions that I wasn't interested in the finer points of who he is. You have shown me so much mercy! You have brought us together in emotional and spiritual intimacy that far outstrips the challenge of change that it took to get here. I thank You, Father, for the amazing privilege of marriage being the only picture in the earth of Jesus' relationship with the Church. I pray that in ever-increasing measure Barry and I will be a picture of that, as he exemplifies Christ's sacrificial love and leadership while, by Your grace, I am his adoring bride who responds to him with strength, beauty, wisdom, submission, and respect, picturing the response of Your people to You. To Your name be the glory! In Jesus' name, amen.

How does Tamra live out being a helper to Barry, who is both an entrepreneur businessman and a church-planting pastor? When he is working through a business decision of any kind and chooses to talk it over with her, she does two things:

1. She tries to ask good questions that can spur his thinking on the matter.

2. She remembers that she doesn't have to have all the answers. She doesn't want to be a wife who overly challenges or discourages her husband's initiatives in his world of work out of fear of the "what-ifs," so she keeps her confidence ultimately in God.

She comes alongside Barry by showing love and appreciation for his employees, whether through a casual dinner for six, a big Christmas party, or remembering to send a gift when a baby is born. She helps her pastor husband by giving him space and quiet from Friday through Sunday every week while he is preparing for his sermon. She practices the discipline of "limited conversation topics." (She says she still has a long way to go in really applying this one but is working on it!) She tries to be a keen and attentive listener rather than an open fire hydrant, gushing chatter and interrupting. She shares with him "what she sees" in ways that ultimately build up their church and the work of the ministry.

I want to close this section with one more example of how a wife can be a helper to her husband—keep in mind that this looks different for every wife.

Recently Jody and I were invited to dinner at the home of his cardiologist. We arrived at 5:00 p.m. with other friends. Chee-Hwa, the doctor's wife, and their four children were there, but not Chris, the doctor. I watched Chee-Hwa as the hours passed. I listened to her conversation when Chris called to say he would be home "sometime." How was Chee-Hwa a helper to her husband? She didn't gripe and complain to him or to their guests. Instead, she cheerfully served dinner and had their children perform for us on the cello and violin. Chris arrived during the performance, three-and-a-half hours late.

Chee-Hwa is a professional pianist who taught music at a university. She says living the life of a single career woman was a breeze compared with being a helper and mother to four. Chee-Hwa is still a professional musician, but I love watching how she is also becoming a professional at her "second" career as a wife.

Tamra and Chee-Hwa are imperfect wives, just like you and me, but they have thought intentionally about how to fulfill their calling as a wife, which is one way a wife fills her husband's respect gap and invites emotional intimacy.

If you are feeling brave, ask your husband this question: *What one thing can I do today that would make me a better helper to you?*

In the next insights, we'll look at additional ways you can invite emotional intimacy with your husband.

Insight 4: FILL HIS GAPS WITH ENCOURAGEMENT AND RESPECT

A wife can do many things to her husband's gaps, but I want to look at two that speak loudly to me: *encouragement* and *respect*.

"Encourage one another and build up one another" (1 Thess. 5:11). The Hebrew word for encouragement means literally to "stir up," "to provoke," "to incite people in a given direction." One dictionary defines *encouragement* as "the act of inspiring others with renewed courage, renewed spirit, or renewed hope." I love that. As a wife, I encourage Jody on our journey together through the seasons of life by putting my arm around him, walking with him, and whispering words that spur him on to be more, to be all God desires him to be as a man, a husband, a father. When I encourage

Jody, I put courage into him to keep on keeping on when life is hard. And he does the same for me.

I see emotional intimacy as entering into each other's life and hearing not just the words but the heart. This last year, Jody entered into my emotional space and heard my heart. He saw my unshed tears. I'd had a very difficult brain day—that means nothing clicked, not thoughts or words, and I felt disoriented living my own life. I was discouraged and just plain sad. I walked in the door and saw a vase with pink roses and a card. My heart jumped. *Who sent the roses?* The card propped against the beautiful roses said, "Honey, I don't think I realized how hard the whole brain injury thing is for you. I know you work hard not to complain but I watch you—you're having to relearn life. I respect you so much for trusting God and wanting to honor Him in all this."

Jody lived Ephesians 4:29. God speaks in this verse in contrasts:

> *Let no unwholesome word proceed from your mouth, but only such a word as is good for edification according to the need of the moment, so that it will give grace to those who hear.*

Do not speak dirty, rotten garbage words, literally.

Do speak words that build up, meet the need of the moment, and give grace to the hearer.

Jody's words poured courage into me; they cradled my sad heart. *Jody respects me; he thinks I'm honoring God.* The tears of frustration I had held back all day now poured out as tears of hope.

I love the way *The Message* renders Ephesians 4:29: "Say only what helps, each word a gift." Can you imagine how your husband would feel if each word you spoke to him was a gift? You would certainly be inviting him into emotional intimacy with you! *Lord, pierce that thought into my heart and mind. Let me live today speaking only "gift words" to my husband.*

Jody loves to invite our ministry team couples over for dinner in the relaxed atmosphere of our home so that he can really get to know them. My introverted husband has commented over and over how much this little act of helping encourages him. When I pour encouragement into Jody by my words and actions, I am giving him a source of fresh energy.

Dr. Henry H. Goddary discovered that encouragement is actually an energy source, which can be measured in the laboratory. He pioneered studies using an instrument devised to measure fatigue. When an assistant would say to the tired child at the laboratory instrument, "You're doing fine, John," the boy's energy curve would soar. Discouragement and faultfinding were found to have an opposite effect, which could also be measured.[6] So when you encourage your husband, it pours courage and renewed strength in him, and when you criticize and complain, it drains him of courage and energy.

Respect will also have a powerful effect on your husband: "And let the wife see that she respects and reverences her husband" (Eph. 5:33 AB). Does your husband really need respect from you? Listen to wives' comments about the worst thing they did for their marriage:

I loved him the way I wanted to be loved. For many years he needed respect and so many other things from me, and I rarely met his needs. (Married twenty-six years)

I took too long to figure out how important unconditional respect is to my husband. (Married thirty-one years)

I did not respect and honor my husband—when I finally did after eighteen years of marriage, he became my God-given spiritual cover. (Married thirty-two years)

I don't respect my husband in word and action. I talk negatively about him to others. (Married fourteen years)

If those comments don't convince you, consider doing the following exercise.[7] Get out a piece of paper and pen and find a quiet place. Spend ten or fifteen minutes making a list of things you respect about your husband. Next, wait until your husband isn't busy or distracted, and say, "I was thinking about you today and several things about you that I respect, and I just want you to know that I respect you." After saying you respect him, do not wait for any response (this is very important!). Just smile and quietly start to leave the room. One woman said that after telling her husband she respected him, she turned to leave but she never made it out the door. He practically shouted, "What things?" Because this wife had made her list, she had things on the tip of her tongue to share with him. After she was finished, he said, "Wow! Hey, can I take the family out to dinner?"[8]

I have force-fed my favorite translation of Ephesians 5:33 into my brain because it makes the word *respect* come alive.

> *And let the wife see that she respects and reverences her husband [that she notices him, regards him, honors him, prefers him, venerates, and esteems him; and that she defers to him, praises him, and loves and admires him exceedingly]. (AB)*

Could the word *respect* really embody all of those words? These are strong words: *honor, prefer, esteem, praise, love,* and *admire exceedingly.* Is this really what God asks a wife to do? Yes, my friend, it is. I often pray, asking God to make this verse a reality in my relationship with Jody. My prayer sounds something like this:

> *My Father, this verse says so much. Please show me how to notice Jody, to regard him. In what ways can I honor him, prefer him above others? Lord, what does it look like to venerate and esteem him? As I go through these words, I'm thinking, How does one*

woman do all this? Only You can show me. I want to praise Jody in words that will speak to him—reveal to me what they are. I want to love and admire my man exceedingly. I want to express respect to him in all these ways today.

Writing out this prayer makes me sigh. It is so much, yet I am grateful that this one verse explains respect so well. Having these words in my heart and mind has encouraged me more than any other one thing in living out respect.

During a difficult time in her marriage, a wise wife wrote the following acrostic to help her remember how to show her husband respect:

Revere
Esteem
Submit
Prize
Enjoy
Comfort
Trust

My friend, learn how to respect your husband. This is important to him and to your marriage. Learning to respect your unique man is an art. Learning to meet his deep needs is a skill. It is a challenge that takes a lifetime. And when you pour encouragement and respect into your husband, you invite emotional intimacy.

Insight 5: WHO WILL FILL MY GAPS?

Maybe you are thinking, *Great, Linda—I'm supposed to be this super helper to my husband. I work hard to fill his respect gap, but isn't he supposed to do something for me?* Good question.

The commands to a husband are difficult; I believe those are more difficult to live out than the commands to a wife. When you read Ephesians 5:21–33, you know that God commands husbands to fill their wife's love gap. A husband is to love his wife as Christ loved the Church, which means laying down his life for her (v. 25). That is the ultimate love.

Husbands are also to love their wife's body as much as they love their own bodies (v. 28–29). That command confused me at first, and I thought, *Jody loves the curves of my body, not his body!* But then I remembered that many men get *very* concerned if they are sick. When a man is sick, sickness is serious. The verse means that Jody is to be as concerned about my headache as he is about his own headache, as caring about my sinus infection as about his stuffed-up head. This puts a different light on this verse.

But what do you do when your husband doesn't fill your love gap? What do you do with your unmet needs? What if you do all you know to do to get closer to him—you accept and act on God's call to you as your husband's helper and to pour encouragement and respect into him, but he doesn't care, doesn't try, and doesn't move toward you?

That is hard, very hard. If that is your situation, you may be thinking, *Easy for you to say, Linda. Your husband loves the Lord and loves you.* And you are right. I am blessed with a husband who loves the Lord and who loves me. But that doesn't mean our marriage has been easy.

When I said, "I do," I made an unconditional commitment to an imperfect person. I also made a commitment to God that I would seek to be Jody's helper—to meet his needs rather than to have my needs met. The world shouts, "It's all about you; get your needs met!" Jesus, the Christ, brings a different perspective: "I came not to be served but to serve" (Matt. 20:28, author's paraphrase). Jesus came to lay down His life that we might be free. Then He says to me, *Linda, will you follow in My steps and be Jody's helper? Will you seek to serve and not to be served?*

At a point in time, I said yes to this commitment, but I have to reaffirm my decision. Making this choice has freed me from expecting Jody to fill my love gap, and accept me, encourage me … the list goes on and on. When my dearly beloved understands me, shows me affection, or loves me sacrificially, it is a gift of God, given to me through my husband. It is not my right. Changing my perspective from *my right* to *God's gift* has enabled me more and more to seek to meet Jody's needs, and this is exactly what God wants me to do … what He wants every wife to do.

It took me years to get this perspective. Michelle is a young woman who learned much more quickly than I did. After she and her husband, Josh, had been married for a couple of years, Michelle began to feel depressed and unhappy. She married believing Josh would meet all her needs for love, acceptance, and security. She thought she would be married to someone who would always be on her side, adore and love her no matter what she did, and understand her completely, even when she didn't understand herself.

When this wasn't the case, Michelle became confused, frustrated, and angry. She thought, *Maybe I'm not trying hard enough,* so she worked hard to do all the things for Josh that communicated love to her, like writing little love notes and buying him surprises. She tried harder and harder at losing weight, cleaning house, and memorizing facts about current events, so she would be interesting. When trying harder didn't work, Michelle tried confronting Josh on how he wasn't loving her enough. She also tried appealing to his sympathy by crying and being pitiful. Nothing worked.

I believe that what God revealed to Michelle will encourage you, as it did me. She sent me the following in an email:

> *I vividly remember the afternoon when I concluded that Josh either would not or could not love me the way I needed to be loved. It just was not going to happen. I was furious at God. I told Him that I had prayed for my mate since I was in the ninth grade. I had prayed about my engagement to Josh. I had tried to follow God every step of the way. God, better than anyone, knew how I needed to be loved. How could He do this to me? I remember hitting my bed in anger and crying. As I sat there it became clear to me that somebody was going to have to give in this argument. It was going to be God or me, and chances were good it was going to be me.*

I knew that God was asking me to change. I needed to give those needs and desires to Him as a sacrifice and trust Him to meet them, however He chose. That is easy to say, but overwhelming to actually do. I felt as if God was literally asking me to cut my heart out and give it to Him. (On top of that, I had no anesthesia, and I had to do the surgery myself!) To be loved and cared for the way I had dreamed in marriage was what I had lived for all my life. To give up hope of having it seemed like giving up my life. It was like a death. I lay across my bed and cried and cried until I was exhausted both physically and emotionally.

Then it dawned on me that this is what it means in a practical way to deny myself and follow Christ. This is what it means to lose my life for His sake (Matt. 16:25). I decided to write out in my journal the specific things that I was giving to God that day. These are a few of the things that were on my list:

- *The belief that my marriage would make me secure.*
- *The belief that my marriage would completely fill my need for love.*
- *The idea that any human being can love me completely without ever wavering.*
- *The belief that my emotional maturity, my fulfillment and happiness was Josh's responsibility.*
- *The belief that Josh's emotional maturity, fulfillment, and happiness was my responsibility.*

After I wrote these things out in my journal I experienced peace and joy for the first time in weeks. I was even feeling humorous. I wrote in my journal, "Now, God, is there anything else You want, as long as I have the incision open here?"

As I look back over the years since that day, I see it as a real turning point. My mission in marriage was changed from getting my needs met to letting God teach me how to love Josh, just for the sake of obeying and pleasing God. This has been really hard. Many times the decision to love is very private. There is no one to applaud or to say, "Boy, Michelle, that was really an unselfish thing to do." There is no one there who knows how much it hurts in that moment to choose to love, except God.

I have learned and I am still learning how to tell God about my needs and trust Him to meet them. He does meet them in surprising ways. I am also learning that as I love Josh without pressuring him with expectations, God has been teaching him how to better love me and meet my needs.

Michelle expressed it well. God wants you to concentrate on how to please your husband. You have found him, your one unique man to love, an original unlike any other. You are on this marriage journey together, and you are the one close to his heart; you are the one who knows his deep needs. You don't have to fill the respect gap of any other man, only this one, but it can take a lifetime to intimately know, understand, and love your man.

> *Do nothing from selfishness or empty conceit, but with humility*
> *of mind let every wife regard her husband as more important*
> *than herself; do not merely look out for your own personal*
> *interests, but also for the interests of your husband.*

Philippians 2:3–4, my paraphrase

Insight 6: A WIFE CAN SET THE STAGE FOR INTIMACY

When I accept God's call on my life to be Jody's helper and apply "helping" specifically to him, I am creating an atmosphere of sweetness in our relationship. When sweetness reigns in our marriage, there is a deep emotional understanding, a flowing of tenderness and gentle touch. Soft words of love and silly smiles of connection abound. But when I put my rights over my husband's, I stifle that sweetness.

I shared my thoughts with Jody about the joy we had when emotional sweetness hovered. I asked him, "Honey, what do you think is the opposite of sweetness?"

His answer literally astounded me: "Loneliness."

Lord, is that how Jody feels on days when our love grates, when my voice has irritation to it because I am irritated?

The Lord's whisper of, *Yes, Linda, that is how he feels,* sent me once again to my Thankful Journal, and I wrote:

> *Today, Lord, how can my love be patient? I want to:*
> - *Give the grace I give to a friend to my lover/my friend.*
> - *Get behind his eyeballs and see the today of life as he sees it.*
> - *Be as understanding of his weaknesses as I was the first year of our marriage.*

It is a challenge for every wife to do her part to create emotional intimacy with her husband. It is especially difficult for American military wives. They are some of the most incredible women I know. Their husbands are away for a year or more at a time—in Iraq, Afghanistan, or another faraway country. These wives are alone a lot, and it is not easy.

Krista is such a wife. She made it her goal to fill her husband's gaps. Her loving plan poured encouragement, respect, and hope into her husband, Caleb. I'll let her tell you her story.

> *When I was ten years old, I was abducted on the way to school and sexually abused the whole day. In the evening I was able to get away. This day defined my life in many ways—I was told I wouldn't be able to have children.*

I met Caleb after he had finished medical school. He told me that he had had testicular cancer, and that even though he was declared healed, the doctors said he wouldn't be able to have children. It sounds crazy but on our second date we told each other that we couldn't have children. This was the medical story. God's story is that Caleb and I gave birth to three precious children.

Caleb became a brigade surgeon in the military and went to Iraq. After six months, he was coming home for two weeks—and I was excited. I listened to friends as their husbands came home for the two-week furlough, and it was, "Oh, this is my chance.... He'll watch the kids, and I'm going to the spa." God let me wrestle about this, and I cried out to Him and said, Lord, You orchestrate these two weeks.

To prepare spiritually, I prayed about my goal: Lord, I want to fill my husband up to full and overflowing—only You can show me how to fill him up, spirit, soul, and body. Only You can show me how to fill him up so he's ready to go back to war for six more months.

God speaks personally, and He is a very practical God. I asked Him to plan these special two weeks, and I did what He led me to do to prepare for our time together. To prepare practically:

- *I wrote Caleb and asked him everything he wanted to eat while home. I shopped and bought everything needed for the two weeks.*
- *I bought seven bedroom outfits in seven different colors.*
- *I arranged with a friend whose husband was also home to swap children so we would each have twenty-four hours alone with our husband.*
- *I bought a massage book and studied it.*

When the children and I picked Caleb up at the airport, we brought him fresh-smelling civilian clothes to put on. When soldiers come home from war, they reek of death and destruction. It is horrible beyond anything I can describe to you. After changing, Caleb threw his uniform into the back of the van. When we came out of the restaurant, the stench in the van was so foul we had to air it out before we could drive home.

We got the kids in bed and sat on the couch and made out—just because we could! Even then I am saying, Lord, show me how to love him. Caleb's love language is physical touch, and the Lord had whispered to me, "Give him a bath." So into the tub Caleb went. I straddled the tub with my big sponge and began to cleanse the smells of war. And as I washed the odor of war away, I prayed to cleanse his soul from the spirit of death and destruction. As I washed his head and hair, I prayed, Lord, let nothing he has thought harm him. As I wiped his eyes, I prayed, Lord, let nothing he has seen stay in his heart. As I washed his ears, I prayed, Lord, let nothing he has heard touch his spirit. I washed and prayed over every part of my husband, begging God that nothing would take root, that all evil would be washed away.

After this spiritual and physical cleansing, I got in the bath with him, and then I said, "Honey, pick a color." The poor man had no idea what was going on so I told him seven colors and said, "Just pick one … you'll be glad you did."

I put on the bedroom outfit in his choice of color, and we made love five times in the first twenty-four hours he was home—and one of those lovemaking sessions lasted two hours! We cracked up—was this even physically possible?

During our twenty-four hours alone we pulled down the shades and said, "We can walk around naked. We can do anything we want—such joy … such freedom … such delight!"

One day I put my new massage techniques into practice and gave Caleb a full-body massage. He was so relaxed he slept for two hours. His comment, "That was amazing. I never slept like that in Iraq."

I had asked God to reveal how to love my special man for two weeks. I love how God answers so tenderly and specifically when we cry out to Him.

- *I cooked Caleb's favorite meals.*
- *Paraded in seven outfits in seven colors.*
- *Gave him a physical and spiritual cleansing.*
- *Became his personal massage therapist.*

Our two weeks were a supernatural feast of intimacy with the Lord and with one another.

But the day came when my husband and the children's father had to get on a plane again and fly off to the death and destruction of war. Had I loved him, spirit, soul, and body, so he was ready to return to war? Three days after he got back, he emailed me and said, "Thank you for the best two weeks of my life."

Krista created a stage where emotional and sexual intimacy could flourish. Her story is one of the most beautiful I have ever heard. She asked God, "How can I be a helper to Caleb during these two weeks?" Her focus was giving to him, but I think she received joy, love, appreciation, and delight in return.

You are called to be your husband's helper, but to do that you need help—help that only the Divine Helper can give. For a husband to love his wife with a sacrificial love is impossible—impossible unless the Holy Spirit gives him the power. For a wife to respect her husband unconditionally is also impossible—impossible unless the Holy Spirit gives her power.

Cry out to God! Fall to your knees and ask Him to give you the creativity, the power, the knowledge to be the helper He created you to be to your unique man.

Dangerous Prayer!

Lord, change my selfish heart. Work in me so I can truly learn to be a helper to my husband. Show me what encouragement and respect look like to him. I want to do my part to create emotional intimacy with him.

What Is It Like to Make Love with Me?

Certainly sex can be "I will do that for you if you will
do this for me," but what a lonely arrangement.
A caress should say "I love you," not pay off a debt. An
embrace should fill the heart as well as the arms.
Hugh and Gayle Prather, *Notes to Each Other*

Thrills come at the beginning and do not last....
Let the thrill go ... and you will find you are
living in a world of new thrills.
C. S. Lewis, *Mere Christianity*

Couples who frequently pray together are twice as likely as those who
pray less often to describe their marriages as being highly romantic....
But get this—married couples who pray together are ninety
percent more likely to report higher satisfaction with their
sex lives than couples who don't pray together....
Prayer, because of the vulnerability it
demands, also draws a couple closer.
Les and Leslie Parrott, "Skimming the Surface?"
Marriage Partnership

> *The camaraderie of best friends who are also lovers*
> *seems twice as exciting and doubly precious.*
> Ed Wheat, *Love Life for Every Married Couple*

Insight 1: HOW DID WE GET WHERE WE ARE?

Have you ever heard a story and wondered if it was true or the figment of a lively imagination? This story caused me to wonder, but I've been assured that it actually happened. The names have been changed to protect the innocent and guilty, and as you read the story you will see why.

Jacki and Jon were engaged. They promised themselves they would wait to have sex until they were married, but as the wedding got closer, restraining themselves seemed impossible. They wanted to obey God—they wanted His best—but this was beyond hard. People's comments didn't help. "You mean you're both virgins? That's awful. Your honeymoon won't be any fun. You should sleep together now so you can enjoy your honeymoon."

Motivated by this advice and weakened by their own strong desires, Jacki and Jon set aside their resolve and decided to take the plunge. Jacki lived with her parents, so she and Jon chose a time when the house would be empty. When they had progressed to the "sans clothing" stage, the phone rang. Jacki answered and rolled her eyes as she listened to her mother's voice. Yes, she would go downstairs and turn off the iron that her mother had left on. Feeling playful, Jon laughingly picked up his naked fiancèe and carried her down the stairs. Halfway down, he tripped, and she ended up at the bottom of the stairs with a broken leg. As Jon rushed to Jacki's side, relatives and friends burst through the door shouting, "Surprise! We're having a party for you! We called and asked you to turn off the iron to be sure you were home!"

You can guess who was surprised. How do you explain that you really haven't "done it" yet? That the only reason you are both naked is because you were afraid sex was going to be such a scary deal—that you had to perform just right—and you didn't want your honeymoon ruined? Who would believe that? Jacki hobbled down the aisle a few weeks later with a cast on her leg.

It makes me sad that this couple felt so pressured about sex. Has our society so indoctrinated us through the fantasy machines of movies and television that Christian young people are afraid to wait for marriage because they fear they won't be able to perform adequately? Don't the women of the twenty-first century understand that the wedding night is only the beginning of a lifetime of growing together in the intimacy of sexual love?

This story is just one of many I've heard that bear truth to this fact: God's women are confused about sexual intimacy in marriage. Since writing *Intimate Issues* in 1999 with my wonderful friend Lorraine Pintus, I have talked to thousands of women of all ages about their sexual intimacy in marriage. It's not just unmarried women who are confused; wives are as well. Many wives are:

- Afraid of sexual intimacy
- Disappointed in sexual intimacy
- Hindered by guilt over their wrong choices
- Confused over what a godly and sensuous wife looks like
- Ready to forget the whole thing

Where did these confused, disappointed, fearful, guilt-ridden mind-sets originate? How did we get where we are?

I believe that our distorted ideas about sexual intimacy are due to three intimacy robbers: Satan, the media, and the Church. Let me explain.

Intimacy robber 1: Satan. If I had to name the top intimacy robber for women today, it would be the Enemy of your soul. *Devil* is a translation of the Greek word *diabolos,* which means "slanderer" or "accuser." The Devil is a murderer and a liar (John 8:44), an accuser (Rev. 12:10), and an adversary (1 Peter 5:8). He's also called the thief, and one of his targets is your sexuality. He tells you lies like, "You can't be godly if you are abandoned and intoxicated by delight in your husband's caresses," and "God just isn't pleased with you in the bedroom; you better be uptight, prim. Don't get carried away."

Lies, lies, lies. Straight from the mouth of the Liar.

Two of Satan's greatest lies are:

1. If you made mistakes in this area, forget it. There is no hope for you.

2. If evil was done to you by others, forget it. There is no hope for you.

The Liar sneers, "You blew it—look at all the sexual partners you've had. Remember that abortion? Sex can never be good for you. You're used goods, honey. Give up—your sexuality is beyond repair...."

But the Redeemer declares, "Yes, My child, you blew it, but it is for this that I died. I took all your sexual sin on Me. YOU ARE FORGIVEN! YOU ARE FREE! Now, My daughter, delight in your freedom—listen to My Word. It is truth."

The Liar shouts, "How can there be hope for you? Men used you—abused you. Do you think you can ever think differently about sex? About a man's body? Sex is messy, you are messy—scarred to your core. Give up—there is no hope...."

The Healer comes. He embraces you and tenderly whispers: "I can make *all* things new. Even your sexuality. I love you, precious one. Trust Me!"

Intimacy robber 2: the media. Running a close second to the Liar is the media and culture. Television, books, magazines, billboards, and hundreds of thousands of websites *overemphasize* sex and exploit the female body. Nothing is private. The message is this: sex anytime, anywhere, with anyone—hook up, hop into bed—it's just physical, and it feels sooooooooo good!

Every time Viagra or Cialis ads come on during a football game, I think: *Twelve-year-old boys are snickering about four-hour erections. Young girls are trying to figure out what it all means.* It makes me sad; it makes me sick. If I feel this way, I can only imagine how God feels.

Make no mistake: The media is a fantasy machine. They project a larger-than-life view of sex in order to promote the fantasy. Remember, the goal of the media is to leave you breathless and wide-eyed, not better informed. The cops and robbers don't shoot real bullets in those movies, either. It's an elaborately staged setup.

Lindsey bought into the media's lies. She told me:

> *I see it now. I believed lies. The movies portrayed sex as always steamy, romantic, and fun—pleasure was always off the charts amazing. When it wasn't like this for us, I took a step back from intimacy in my mind and heart. After kids, sex was something I "put up with." I took more steps away. Without saying it out loud, inwardly I gave up and believed we'd never go to a place called "exciting sex."*

Lindsey felt sexual intimacy should always be as exciting as Hollywood's. Other Christian women go the opposite direction. They look at the degradation of sexuality portrayed by the media and, revolted, inwardly choose to believe that sex is something evil and not to be enjoyed. Meanwhile, the second robber—the media—gathers his stolen goods and thinks nothing of those who suffer the loss.

The truth is, your love life is the real thing and, pursued with elan, can provide infinitely better pleasure and intimacy than any manufactured fantasy.

Intimacy robber 3: the Church. The third thief is not so blatant in her actions. Her stealth is disguised with noble words and pious ideas. And in truth, the motivation behind her thefts is not dishonorable. Beginning with the early Church fathers and continuing through the centuries, the Church hoped to stifle immorality and inappropriate sex but instead stifled beautiful and appropriate sex in marriage. Listen to the voices cascading down through the centuries:

- Augustine allowed that sex is good, but that passion and desire are sin.[1]
- "The Holy Spirit leaves the room when a married couple has sex, even if they do it without passion"—Peter Lombard, theologian (circa 1100–1164).
- Martin Luther wrote: "Intercourse is never without sin; but God excuses it by his grace because the estate of marriage is his work."[2]
- In her book of encouragement to new brides, a pastor's wife in the late 1800s gave this sterling advice: "One cardinal rule of marriage should never be forgotten: give little, give seldom and above all give grudgingly. Otherwise what could have been a proper marriage could become an orgy of sexual lust."[3]

Oh, brother! What a positive, exciting, and uplifting picture of sexual intimacy!

The Church gave wrong advice. You probably never heard "Give little, give seldom and above all else, give grudgingly" from a godly pastor's wife, but many Christian wives have been influenced by distorted messages filtered down through the centuries. Sadly, they have adopted an incorrect sexual mind-set without even realizing where they got it.

We've looked at how we got where we are, but what we have to discern is: How do we get where we want to be?

Maybe your sexual intimacy with your husband is already where you want it to be. Your sexual relationship has been a dream—no past mistakes, no harm done to you. You came into marriage excited about sex, and the ride has been incredible. If this is your story, I shout "Hurrah" and rejoice with you! You are blessed. Thank God!

But many women have a different story, and they are nowhere close to where they want to be. With all the confusion and misinformation, what does it look like for you to become God's picture of an exciting lover? How do you exchange these harmful attitudes for God's attitude that you are to enjoy beautiful, free, abandoned delight—and exquisite pleasure—with your husband? The first thing you need to do is this: *Shut your eyes and open your ears.* Refuse to listen to the lies of the Enemy. Stop looking at the media. Refuse to listen to any source that feeds misinformation. Instead, start looking only at God and His viewpoint. And where is His perspective? In His Word. So open your Bible. Open wide your heart. Fling open your spiritual eyes and ears. God has some gifts that He longs for you to open. Each of these gifts will encourage you in answering the Dangerous Question: *What is it like to make love with me?* Keep reading to find out more.

Insight 2: OPEN THE GIFT OF SEXUAL PASSION

Picture in your mind a beautiful, big, shocking-pink gift bag with your name emblazoned across it in gold letters. Your Father God has this gift just for you, and He wants you to open it. What is the gift? Holy, pure, exciting, intoxicating sex.

Listen deeply to God's Word. He declares that He gave you the gift of sexual passion for *intimate oneness* and *pleasure.* Join me in imagining God at His creation. Adam and Eve are created in His image, and Adam has jumped up and down with excitement over the woman God has brought to him. Her skin, her hair, her smile ... Adam is beside himself with joy, but God has one more surprise: "My children, I have designed your bodies so that they can literally become one. I've given you a tangible way to bridge the loneliness you will feel, and to enable you, whenever you choose, to lose yourselves in one another. And as amazing as it seems, this sexual oneness will picture for you the spiritual oneness I want to have with you—a holiness shrouds your sexual intimacy."

While the Genesis record does not mention God saying this to Adam and Eve, the words echo His intent. Does this seem "out there"? It's not. Look with me at Ephesians 5:31–32.

A man [shall] leave his father and mother, and shall cleave to his
wife; and the two shall become one flesh. This mystery is great: but
I speak in regard of Christ and of the church. (ASV)

In verse 31, Paul quotes from Genesis about leaving, cleaving, and becoming one flesh sexually. It is a reference to the act of sexual intercourse. Then Paul expounds on the great mystery of sexual oneness in verse 32. It's as if he says, "My children, revel in the intimacy, delight in the ecstasy, and when you experience this closest union on earth, lift your eyes and realize this is the degree of spiritual union God longs to have with you."

Do you understand? Do you see? God's gift to you contains a physical joy that speaks of a spiritual joy. His holiness infuses your intimate oneness with your husband. Close your eyes, bow to Him in worship, and thank Him for His gift.

God gave you the gift of passion so that you and your husband can experience intimate oneness. He also gave it to you so you could share exquisite pleasure.

God is for pleasure! He is very specific so that we know His heart and see what is good for our hearts. Let's look at two passages that declare God's perspective on sexual pleasure.

The first passage is from Proverbs 5. This is instruction from a father to his son, begging him to stay away from sexual pleasure outside of marriage (5:1–14). Then in the verses following, the father entices his son by saying there are unbelievable, amazing, exquisite sexual pleasures within marriage.

Drink water from your own cistern
   And fresh water from your own well....
Let your fountain be blessed,
   And rejoice in the wife of your youth.
As a loving hind and a graceful doe,

Let her breasts satisfy you at all times;
Be exhilarated always with her love. (vv. 15, 18–19)

What do you see in these verses?

I see pleasure.

I see delight.

I see fun.

I see freedom, abandonment, intoxication, ecstasy.

What do these words say to me as a wife?

I am to be a continual, flowing fountain of pleasure for my husband. I am to be a loving doe, a graceful deer; so cute, so soft that my husband wants to reach out and touch, to fondle and cuddle me. And there's more.

God's Word encourages my husband and yours to:

1. Let your wife's breasts satisfy you always.

2. Be captivated, exhilarated, intoxicated always with her sexual love.

This straightforward passage doesn't leave much to the imagination, does it? As a wife, I am to be a continual, delightful source of refreshing pleasure to this husband I love. I am to intoxicate him with my sexual love—always. That means every year of our marriage. Of course, all that I am to be and do goes for him, too. He is to intoxicate me as well. Amen and amen.

I see holiness in this passage. God delights in encouraging the husband and wife to rejoice in their sexual intimacy. He places His stamp of approval on it—making it holy—so I add holiness to the pleasure, delight, fun, freedom, abandonment, intoxication, and ecstasy I see in these verses. I bow and worship my God. He combines His holiness with sexual pleasure.

Now for the second passage that describes the pleasure a husband and wife are to experience in their sexual union. Put on your sunglasses—this will make your eyes pop. It is beautiful. It is sensuous. It is romantic. It is erotic. Okay, did I just apply words like *sensuous* and *erotic* to God's Word? Yep, I did. Those are the words that apply.

> *How beautiful are your sandaled feet,*
>   *O queenly maiden.*
> *Your rounded thighs are like jewels,*
>   *the work of a skilled craftsman.*
> *Your navel is perfectly formed*
>   *like a goblet filled with mixed wine.*
> *Between your thighs lies a mound of wheat*
>   *bordered with lilies.*
> *Your breasts are like two fawns,*
>   *twin fawns of a gazelle.*
> *Your neck is as beautiful as an ivory tower.*
> *Your eyes are like the sparkling pools in Heshbon*
>   *by the gate of Bath-rabbim.*
> *Your nose is as fine as the tower of Lebanon*
>   *overlooking Damascus.*
> *Your head is as majestic as Mount Carmel,*
>   *and the sheen of your hair radiates royalty.*
>   *The king is held captive by its tresses.*
> *Oh, how beautiful you are!*
>   *How pleasing, my love, how full of delights!*
> *You are slender like a palm tree,*
>   *and your breasts are like its clusters of fruit.*
> *I said, "I will climb the palm tree*
>   *and take hold of its fruit."*
> *May your breasts be like grape clusters,*
>   *and the fragrance of your breath like apples.*
> *May your kisses be as exciting as the best wine,*
>   *flowing gently over lips and teeth. (Song 7:1–9 NLT)*

In these verses Solomon describes his bride's dancing feet and progresses up her scantily clothed body. Either she is nude or in a shimmering, sheer garment, because Solomon can see every part of her body. He comments on her swaying thighs, saying they are like jewels, the perfect work of a skilled craftsman. Her "navel" is filled with mixed wine. (Sorry, but *navel* is a wrong translation. The translator could not bring himself to say the part of her body between her thighs and belly. Bet you can figure it out for yourself.) Her breasts are like twin fawns (once again, we see the imagery of a soft, touchable baby deer). The lover mentions his bride's breasts three times in verses 3, 7, and 8. He is delighted and intoxicated with the glory of his wife's curvy body as she passes before his eyes.

What do I see in these verses?

I see creativity.

I see seduction.

I see sexual adventure.

I see a wife who knows her man.

Solomon's bride knew God created her husband to be aroused through his eyes, so she entices, seduces, and delights him with her body. She knows her body is a gift for her husband.

I hope that as you read of the beauty and holiness in these biblical pictures, you grew excited about traveling with your husband to this place of joy, abandonment, and adventure. If so, you are feeling exactly what God wants you to feel.

If not, you may feel more like Claire, who was initially filled with fear and panic at the thought of journeying to deeper sexual intimacy. Let me share her story with you.

Claire doesn't know who her father is because her mother was with so many men. What's unimaginable to me is that this mother allowed her daughter to be photographed as part of the child pornography industry. Claire says, "I can still hear the photographer's words, 'Now smile, pretty honey … you're such a pretty little thing.' As I became a teenager, I felt viciously robbed of something that was mine to give away. I was ruined, scarred, and knew I could never get married."

When Claire's husband, Derek, first asked her to marry him, she told him no. But he wouldn't give up and asked until she finally said, "Yes, I'll marry you and just have to deal with the sex part." On their wedding day, Claire didn't experience the normal anticipation and excitement that a bride should feel. Instead she felt like "a vacant carcass dressed up in a pretty white dress."

Her incredible man didn't scare easily, and it was a good thing, because when they made love, Claire had panic attacks. She knew she wasn't being raped, but couldn't get over feeling used. She had a long list of places Derek couldn't touch, things she wouldn't do. This was their sex life for several years. She cried out to the Lord for help. *Do something, God. I'll do anything.*

Claire signed them up for a Family Life "Weekend to Remember," where they had to rate each other on passion. Derek rated her as a 2 on a scale of 10, but she knew in her heart she was a minus 2. At that conference Claire bought a copy of *Intimate Issues*. I asked her to tell you what happened next.

> *When I read the title of the first chapter, "What Does God Think About Sex?" my first thought was, God thinks about sex? Why would He do that? I read the chapter and said out loud to God, This can't be true. I determined to read it a second time and looked up all the Scripture references and wrote them down. God, IT IS TRUE! What have I done?*
>
> *I began meeting with a spiritual mentor and reading the Song of Solomon. I told my mentor, "Either every word of the Bible is true, or none of it is true. I can't pick and choose what I accept." I remember reading Song of Solomon 4:16, and I was shocked. I asked my mentor what this verse meant, and she said, "What do you think it means?" I admitted that it looked like it*

was talking about oral sex between the bride and groom, but that couldn't be true. After all, I had told my husband that oral sex wasn't just wrong ... it was a horrid sin.

The more I read God's Word, the more I saw His picture of beauty and delight in sexual intimacy. But how could I get there? I had told God, If it is in Your Word, I'll believe it and do it. I embraced God's view of sex in my mind and heart and told God I longed for His hand of blessing over us. So I re-created our wedding night. I sent our kids to some friends, pulled our mattress into the living room, and set out candles and draped fabric over the bed to create a canopy.

Derek walked into the dream he thought would never be his reality and heard these words from the wife he had sacrificially loved all these years: "Honey, I've been concentrating for these years on how I was robbed, but I see now that you were severely robbed too. I never fully gave myself to you. Tonight I give you all of me. My body is yours to touch, kiss, fondle in any way you desire—and your body is mine."

That night I took what was mine and gave my husband what was his.

My friend Claire is my hero, a military wife I deeply respect. She cried out to the Lord for help and said, "I'll do anything." She made a secret choice to believe God's perspective on sex, and then she put into practice what she had learned by re-creating their wedding night.

Claire makes me ask hard questions. I didn't suffer sexual abuse. I didn't have my mind and body scarred. But do I seek God's truth about my sexual relationship like Claire did? Do I take hard steps because they are the right steps? Do you?

God gave the gift of sexual passion. It is His gift to you. Opening this gift will encourage your heart and bring you a step closer to being able to answer the question, *What is it like to make love with me?* with this response: "My husband is blessed to have me as his lover."

Insight 3: OPEN THE GIFT OF GOD'S BLESSING

Carly came up to me at an Intimate Issues Conference and said, "Linda, we have a big picture of Jesus over our bed. Every time we make love, we turn the picture around. It just doesn't seem right to have Jesus watching!" Right … and turning the picture around is sure to keep God out of the bedroom!

There is probably a little of this woman in all of us. No matter how we twist our mind around it, sex just seems too earthy to really have God's blessing. The sights, the sounds of sex, just don't square with the spiritual.

Did you know that God gives His blessing on your sexual oneness with your husband? Picture a shimmering violet gift bag, your name written across it in deep purple letters. This gift is for you, God's daughter. The gift of His blessing frees you to give yourself permission for passion.

We see God's blessing beautifully displayed in the Song of Solomon. In chapter 4 the bride and groom have just consummated their marriage. Their lovemaking has been steamy, very steamy. Listen to the bride's invitation to her lover. Somehow I don't think you'll have trouble figuring out what the word *garden* refers to.

> *Awake, north wind!*
> *Rise up, south wind!*
> *Blow on my garden*
> *and spread its fragrance all around.*
> *Come into your garden, my love;*
> *taste its finest fruits. (Song 4:16 NLT)*

The new husband answers that he has come into his garden and been enraptured with its delicacies (Song 5:1). Then something unexpected happens. A third presence is in the bridal chamber. The One who enters into this sacred chamber is the couple's Creator God. As He lovingly walks over to the bridal bed, the bride and groom lay naked and unashamed in one another's arms, delighting in the afterglow of lovemaking. It is as if their Holy God extends His hand of blessing over them and declares a benediction: "Eat, friends; drink and imbibe deeply, O lovers" (Song 5:1).[4]

Oh, I love God's blessing! In Hebrew, it literally means "to feast." The Almighty, Holy One of heaven and earth says:

> *Have a love feast!*
> *Eat! Drink! Taste deeply of the exquisite pleasures of loving one*
> * another.*
> *Enjoy My gift to the fullest.*
> *I bless your sexual intimacy.*

The Holy God, the Redeemer and Healer, blesses *your* earthy, naked, and unashamed intimacy and ecstasy. Will you receive His personal blessing for you? Jesus' picture can stay over the bed. God sees. God knows. God blesses.

Are you wondering, *How can my husband and I receive God's blessing?* If so, it is not difficult. The next time you and your husband make love, as you are basking in the afterglow of your oneness, imagine together that your Creator walks over to your bed, extends His hand of blessing over you and says, "Feast, lovers! Taste deeply of the exquisite pleasures of loving one another." Thank Him for His blessing on your intimacy. (If you feel your husband could not enter into this blessing, you, alone, can imagine God coming to bless you and receive His hand of blessing.)

I have been surprised and excited to discover what happens when women open the gift of God's blessing on their sexual intimacy. Read what happened to Megan.

> *When we married, my husband was a virgin; I was not. Even*
> *when we were dating I often thought, I don't deserve this guy,*

because I'd had sex with several previous boyfriends. I was a Christian and knew that God reserved sexual intimacy for couples in a committed marriage relationship, but I had sex anyway. Then I got pregnant. I was furious! I didn't want a baby now. I had a budding career! Besides, if my mom and dad ever found out, they'd kill me. My boyfriend wanted to make things work, but as I marched off to an abortion clinic, I yelled over my shoulder at him, "Get out of my life. I never want to see you again."

After that I didn't want anything to do with men. Then I met Kirby at our church singles' group. He was such a godly man. We started dating. He made it clear that he was committed to waiting until marriage for sex, and so we did. During the first few years of marriage, sex was pretty good, but as time went by, I realized that I was just "going through the motions." After we had kids, my desire for sex all but vanished. I didn't understand this until a Right to Life Sunday at church, when they showed a picture of an eight-week-old baby in the womb. The baby waved her tiny hand, and it was as if she called out to me: "Hi, Mom." I lost it. The abortion had been years earlier, but it wasn't until that moment that I'd come face-to-face with what I'd done: I'd killed my own baby. I grieved for weeks. I cried out to God to forgive me. I'd asked Him to forgive in the past, and I believe He had, but truthfully, I'd never forgiven myself. I don't think I could have because I hadn't faced the breadth and depth of my sin. I'd stuffed my emotions and punished myself with subconscious thoughts like: I don't deserve this man. I don't deserve to enjoy sex because I am such a horrible person.

Grieving the full impact of my sin brought me to a place of healing. I actually fell more deeply in love with Jesus because I understood more fully what my sin had cost Him. And, I fell more deeply in love with my husband because he hadn't condemned me. It took many

more years, but finally, I gave myself permission for passion. My hus-
band will tell you that this decision has made all the difference in the
world. I'm a free woman now, both in bed and outside of it.

Megan makes me search my heart and ask hard questions. Like many (most?) women, I made wrong choices in the sexual area, but I never suffered the pain of aborting my baby. I didn't live with the consequences of that choice. I didn't have to relearn sexual intimacy after many years of marriage. I watched Megan work hard to come to the place of freedom she lives in today. Do I work as hard? Do you?

Have you received God's blessing? When you do, you'll be another step closer to being able to say that making love to you is *good*.

Insight 4: OFFER THE GIFT OF YOUR BODY

Again, picture a gift. This one is a brilliant red. The name across it is not yours, but your husband's. This gift, which will bring pleasure and delight to you both, is one you will give to him.

The apostle Paul discusses marriage in 1 Corinthians 7, and in the first five verses, he deals with sexual needs. For many years I have seen the beauty of the third gift hidden in the words of 1 Corinthians 7:4. Let's look at how different translations of the Bible render this verse for a deeper understanding of Paul's message:

> *The wife does not have authority over her own body, but the hus-*
> *band does; and likewise also the husband does not have authority*
> *over his own body, but the wife does. (1 Cor. 7:4)*

The *Amplified Bible* adds clarity:

> *For the wife does not have [exclusive] authority and control over*
> *her own body, but the husband [has his rights]; likewise also the*

husband does not have [exclusive] authority and control over his own body, but the wife [has her rights].

The Message adds special beauty and insight:

The marriage bed must be a place of mutuality—the husband seeking to satisfy his wife, the wife seeking to satisfy her husband. Marriage is not a place to "stand up for your rights." Marriage is a decision to serve the other, whether in bed or out.

Wow. One way a wife ministers to her husband is to delight him in the bedroom. I believe this deep ministry begins with giving your body as a gift to your husband. Ideally, a wife gives over authority of her body—gives it as a gift to her husband—on their wedding night, but the reality is that in many cases this does not happen. That was Kathy's story.

After telling her about the beautiful picture in 1 Corinthians 7:4, I asked Kathy if she had ever given over authority of her body to her husband. Her surprised look and silence said no. But I was the one surprised when Kathy told me that on Valentine's Day she had wrapped herself in ribbon and a bow and offered her body as a gift to her husband. She told him that before there had been lots of ifs and noes because she had control of her body, but no longer—her body was his. He was so touched by her gesture that he wept.

A wife can be creative in how she chooses to give her husband the gift of her body.

- Nancy more than shocked her husband when she presented her body in a red bow on their fiftieth anniversary. Jon said it was the best gift he ever received.
- Julie donned her wedding dress and said, "Let's start over.... I want to do it right."
- Mariah felt only a bow went too far for her, so she pinned a yellow bow to her nightgown. Later, her husband asked for the

yellow bow—took it to work and taped it on the inside of his desk, where no one could see it, but his foot would touch it and remind him. Who says men aren't sentimental?

- Becca planned a special romantic weekend away that included lovely music, candles, and a walk by the river. The menu of special food delighted their senses, and the dessert was Becca, wrapped in a chocolate-adorned ribbon.

What does it look like for you to give your body as a gift to your husband?

First, it is a secret choice between you and God. It is an act of your will.

Second, you choose the time, place, and way to give this gift.

What difference will it make in you if you offer this gift to your husband?

If you see your body as "mine," you decide when, where, and how much you'll give to your husband sexually. But if you give your body as a gift to your husband, you'll want him to enjoy the gift. It is *his*—a gift for him to delight in; it is no longer yours. This choice changes everything. For me, the offering of this gift has meant I hold nothing back. I open myself to experience fullness of joy in our sexual intimacy.

Some wives are *very* uncomfortable with the idea of giving authority or control of their body to anyone. Sometimes this stems from plain-old selfishness; however, women who have been sexually abused struggle with anyone having control of their body. Does the idea of your husband having control over your body stir strong emotions inside you? It did for my friend Sadie, and yet God healed her wounds and transformed their marriage. I've asked her to tell you her incredible story.

My husband's chest was wet with tears; mine, not his. This wasn't the first time in our thirteen years of marriage that tears had fallen after making love, but this night was different. These weren't tears flowing out of shame and horrific images of the sexual abuse I'd experienced through my growing-up years. These were tears of joy and thankfulness, springing from a grateful heart to my Savior and Redeemer—the One who could do anything, the One who had healed me.

After Charlie and I were married, it didn't take long for us to realize that intimacy wasn't going to be easy. Our first years of marriage were marked by his need and desire for something I couldn't and didn't want to give. My sexuality had been shattered, and my view of intimacy terribly distorted.

I experienced some healing, enough that we settled for tolerable intimacy. Tolerable was good considering where we had come from. I'd been told that sexually wounded women can't completely recover and to be glad for the progress I had made. There wasn't joy. There wasn't freedom. But at least we could have sex on a semiregular basis, and most times I didn't cry.

After living with tolerable intimacy for a number of years, I felt the Lord begin to nudge my heart to believe Him for something beyond tolerable. I sensed He was asking me to believe that He could take me beyond tolerable to a place of complete freedom. I made a firm resolve that even though I couldn't imagine it, even though I had no strategy of my own to make it happen, I would at least believe my God could do it.

I began to memorize verses from the Song of Solomon that countered the thoughts and feelings that flooded me when Charlie and I were intimate. I went through the motions, silently reciting what I hoped I would actually feel someday. Time and time again I prayed, I cried, I struggled, I doubted, and then asked for faith to believe God again. But a little bit at a time, I began to notice a shift in my thoughts and attitudes. I began to feel desires I hadn't felt before. I began to find pleasure in things that before had made my skin crawl. And I watched my husband's eyebrows go up further and further as he asked things like, "Sooooo, is passionate Sadie here to stay?"

Finally a time came when I was able to make love with my husband without shame. I lay in Charlie's arms and wept over the Lord's mercy toward me. My Healer stood next to me. I felt His smile over me and heard the whisper I had longed for so many years to hear. "My sweet daughter, you are free." Little by little, the Lord did a miracle in my sexuality, and now I am free from tolerable intimacy.

Since these things many months ago, I've been able to stand before my husband wrapped in a bow and truly give myself to him without fear or shame. Charlie and I are delighting in what our Redeemer did for us—the impossible! We are having fun!

Sadie is my hero. She is a prayer counselor and a woman I deeply respect. She believed God for something beyond tolerable sex. She memorized verses from the Song of Solomon. She mentally repeated the verses during sexual intimacy. She prayed, she cried, she struggled and asked God for faith to believe again.

I have not lived through Sadie's deep pain. I have not had to live with tolerable sex. Sadie's journey causes me to search my heart. How many verses have I memorized about Jody's and my intimacy? Do I beg God for more in our sex life? Where would I be if I tried as hard as Sadie to make the most of God's gift of sex? Where would you be?

Giving your body as a gift to your husband is the third step you take so that when you ask yourself, "What is it like to make love with me?" your answer is, "Great! Amazing!"

Insight 5: WHAT DOES EVERYDAY LOVEMAKING LOOK LIKE?
I opened all three gifts, and I can say, "Jody thinks it is fun and exciting to make love with me." Does that mean that every day, through every season, sex is wonderful and that I do it all right? Of course not.

I remember one of the hardest times. Three small children in three years left me beyond exhausted. I was trying to be a good lover but still failed miserably. Jody used every creative bone in his body and made me a very special gift. He created a prescription bottle of fifty-two pills in capsule form, each empty capsule filled, not with medication, but with a creative sexual surprise for each week of the year. The label on the bottle read:

> *For Linda Dillow, prescribed by Dr. Joseph Dillow to alleviate stress.*
>
> > *Take one each week.*

This gift took time to make:

- A trip to a drugstore to get fifty-two capsules. (I can just hear the pharmacist, "What do you want them for?")
- Much time, thought, and creativity to think up and type fifty-two clever ideas, one for each week of the year.
- Much more time and dexterity to cut fifty-two clever ideas into strips and roll them to fit in the tiny capsules. (And this from a husband whose strong suit is not the practical.)

No wonder Jody was disappointed and very hurt when I would forget to take my pill, when my excitement about his special gift was at the same level as my diminished sexual desire.

So I didn't handle this right. And you won't always do things right. But when your husband knows that you *want* to make your sexual intimacy fun and filled with delight, it doesn't hurt so much when you have a "bad sex day" now and then. Lots of times I did do it right. I wrote the following reflection in my journal about the total oneness I felt after a special time of lovemaking.

> *I awoke in the middle of the night. Everything was dark. I could hear Jody breathing next to me. I snuggled up to him and felt the*

warmth again of being close. I lay with my arm around him, reliving the beauty and incredible erotic feelings we had experienced together last night. It was as if our oneness reached a new height and depth. It's all so tied together. Talking and sharing our deep feelings for an hour before making love gave us such an emotional oneness that carried over to our physical oneness.

Experiencing the incredible physical ecstasy with one another is like the "frosting on the cake." It binds us close and adds spice to our spiritual, emotional, and intellectual oneness. I laugh inside at how some would not believe two—not so young people—a missionary and his wife no less!—could so love sex! The lingering feelings of joy and love, of deep satisfaction and peace, fill me with thankfulness for this man, my husband. I find myself here in the dark beside him praising God for His gift of oneness, thanking Him for the delights of sexual joy, and asking Him to show me anew how to cherish this man He has given me.

Lovemaking should include laughter, fun, teasing, joy, and variety. *God gave sex for pleasure, and pleasure is good.* It's not wrong or ungodly to delight in each other's bodies.

Listen to another woman's description of a night of fun and pleasure with her husband:

I woke up this morning laughing to myself. No one ever told me sex could be so much fun. It was hot out last night, so Dan and I decided to pull our mattress out onto our closed-in veranda. We brought glasses of cool lemonade and lay on the mattress sipping our drinks, looking at the stars and talking. I felt like a seventh grader at a slumber party! Dan said he was still hot, so off came his clothes. And then, he decided I'd feel cooler without mine. We buried our faces in our pillows because we were laughing so hard.

Making love in the fresh air was a new sensation. I liked it! We muffled our giggles for fear the neighbors would hear. The sensual feelings were so strong, the slight breeze on our bodies so nice after the hot apartment. I'm glad sex can be such fun and feel so good.

And for those who think life keeps getting in the way …

Our lives are so busy that lately we have to schedule sex—I never read this in a book but it works for us. We put sex down for Friday evening, but Zach's soccer game got rained out and rescheduled for that night. So we rescheduled sex for Saturday morning, but Lucy woke up screaming with an ear infection at 5:00 a.m., and then there was a mad rush to the doctor. On my way out the door I said to my disappointed hubby, "Maybe Sunday night?" But then, Saturday afternoon, a miracle occurred. One child was at a birthday party, and the other two went down for naps at the same time. I grabbed my husband, he grabbed me, and we raced into the bedroom for ten minutes of hot, steamy sex. All that delayed anticipation actually worked magic.

It makes me sad that some Christian women can't enjoy sex on the veranda. The sights, the sounds, the sensations are too *earthy.* And sex in the middle of the afternoon, with kids in the next room? No way! These women can enjoy sex only if they incorporate something spiritual into the physical, such as praying together before making love or singing the doxology together as they orgasm. (Yes, that is for real.)

Please understand. There is nothing wrong with singing praises to God, thanking Him for the gift of sex, or with praying before you make love. These spiritual actions can infuse deep meaning into the physical actions. I just want to emphasize that you don't have to "be spiritual" for God to bless your lovemaking. God has already given you permission to enjoy sex.

It's okay to tease all day long about what's coming later—to laugh, to take a shower together, and to slip into bed or on the floor and pleasure, pleasure, pleasure.

It's okay to grab your husband after he's been away on a trip and love one another quickly, saying, "More to come tonight after the kids are in bed."

It's okay to comfort your husband when he is stressed or depressed by giving love to him physically.

Give yourself permission to enjoy sex. Experiment. Enjoy variety. Don't expect or demand that there always be an hour of emotional sharing before lovemaking. Each time together takes on its own uniqueness, just as each time we talk with our best friend is a different conversation. Find new ways to talk with your husband about your lovemaking so you don't end up in a rut, like poor Emily, who wrote this on my survey:

> *Every time it's the same. He touches me for five minutes, always in the same way. I touch him briefly, he enters me, moves in and out, and it's over. Wham, bam, thank you, ma'am. It's no wonder I don't like sex.*

How awful! I'd be bored too! Lovemaking can be playful and fun, and it can be intense, with tears of deep release and emotion. Incredibly, it can create a child and bring deep oneness or great physical pleasure. It can bring comfort and release tension. Sex is God's gift to His people. Enjoy His gift. Use it wisely, use it freely—and use it often.

Dangerous Prayer!

> *God, I need You! Please show me how to embrace Your perspective from Your Word and give me the courage and strength by Your Spirit to take the hard steps. I long to give my husband the gift of my body, freely and without reservation—to give completely and never take it back again. Please show me practically how to do*

this. I want to be able to answer the Dangerous Question, "What is it like to make love to me?" with, "It is fun, filled with pleasure, and brings deep intimacy to our oneness."

The Worst Things I Did for My Marriage

I was selfish and had an affair. (Married twenty-one years)

I was busy with all that life, family, and ministry generates, so too tired to have energy for sex. (Married twenty-three years)

I settled for a level of intimacy that is far below what I want and what my husband needs. (Married twenty-four years)

I withheld my body from my husband as punishment. (Married twenty-four years)

I withheld sex from my husband because I didn't respect or understand what an important need this was for him. (Married twelve years)

I hung on to the romantic idea of my first boyfriend and lover for twenty-seven years. (Married twenty-seven years)

Been complacent with my husband sexually. (Married thirty years)

Watching porn with my husband. It is not good for our intimacy. (Married nine years)

Innocently "catching up" with an old friend of the opposite sex, which led to confusion and temptation. It made me wonder if maybe I had married the wrong guy. (Married ten years)

Not being sensitive to how long it goes between times of making love. (Married twenty-eight years)

Allowed my past to bind and hinder what God has for me in our sex life. (Married twenty years)

My husband is a doctor and has to get up early for work. He has asked me time and time again to get ready earlier for bed. I don't, and I know it hurts him. (Married thirty-three years)

The Best Things I Did for My Marriage

Been willing to meet his sexual need every other day or at least every third day (no longer) because we've discussed his needs. I had to have a small calendar in the night stand and draw a smiley face on the days we made love. (Married eighteen years)

I am willing and eager for sex every day (or more than once a day!). My question is … why not now? (Married nine years)

I put on my calendar specific times each week for having a rendezvous with my husband to meet his sexual needs, so that he can look forward to our time. If there is going to be a conflict on the schedule for these set times, I arrange another time ahead of the conflict. (Married thirty-seven years)

Realizing that his sexual needs are not selfish, but given from God, and not seeing it as just my duty to fill them, but rather something we experience together. (Married nine years)

Allowing my body to be a source of pleasure and comfort while doing my best to be responsive even when I'm not aroused. (Married five months)

Being willing to work on my issues and be healed of my own sexual sin. (Married thirteen years)

Being honest with my husband about temptation rather than letting it lead me into adultery. (Married ten years)

To ask for what I really need in making love. He really wants to please me. *(Married thirty-three years)*

Got my husband's porn addiction out in the open—been loving and shown grace toward him. *(Married one year)*

Got counseling and came under the healing authority of God's wings! *(Married twenty years)*

Without a doubt the best thing was to agree early in the marriage to the "3 Ds" when we were apart. No **drinking,** no **dancing,** no **developing** friendships with people of the opposite sex. My husband was deployed a lot as a Special Forces soldier. By both of us following the 3 D rules, we never worried about falling into temptation because of long separations. We never wondered and worried. *(Married twenty-three years)*

Why Do I Want to Stay Mad at You?

Over the long run, love's power to forgive is
stronger than hate's power to get even.
Lewis B. Smedes, *Forgive and Forget*

The Puritans called marriage "the little church
within the church." In marriage, every day
you love, and every day you forgive. It is an
ongoing sacrament—love and forgiveness.
Bill Moyers, *The Power of Myth*

Lord, when we are wrong, make us willing to change,
and when we are right, make us easy to live with.
Peter Marshall

Insight 1: IT FEELS GOOD TO HOLD A GRUDGE

Twenty young Texas wives sat around the room, unsure about what to expect. They were from different churches and didn't know each other, but had come together to read an early draft of this book and to do the Bible study. (See page 209.) During the weeks that they met together, the Spirit of

God came in an unusual way and opened their hearts to share some very private things with one another.

The week they studied forgiveness, the leader passed out 3 x 5 cards and asked these wives to write down their answers to the question *Why do I want to stay mad at you?* When I read their answers, I was amazed. These women were tuned into their emotions and their motives.

> *Staying mad is easier than forgiving. Anger justifies and comforts me after an offense. If I remain angry then I have no room in my mind to see fault in myself. If I remain angry, my heart can be so full of blame there's no room for conviction.*

> *U R unrepentant! U cheated—I forgave, I pursued you with God's love—you rejected me! I express my pain, U show no compassion. I stand by your side—U continue 2 pursue other women. I am willing 2 change—to do WHATEVER IT TAKES, U R willing 2 do NOTHING!*

> *I can't forgive you for constantly choosing work over me, because it makes me feel unloved and not appreciated; like you don't care enough about me.*

> *You have hurt me so deeply. I want to hurt you, too. I do not feel safe with you. When I stay mad I can just give up—it's never going to work or be different. It is hopeless. I think my anger gives me power over the hopelessness. If I stay mad, maybe one day it won't hurt so deeply. Maybe one day I won't care.*

> *It seemed staying mad (until reading this Dangerous Question) was my heart's way of protecting itself from being hurt or disappointed over and over again. I now see how much that decision*

robbed so much from our healing and marriage. Now I'm anxious to begin learning how to forgive unconditionally and continuously.

These comments are from young women, some very wounded by their husbands. Several said it felt good to hold a grudge. I'm not a young woman, and I have a wonderful husband. I know God's Word and teach other women about forgiveness, yet there have been many times I wanted to hold on to my "mad" at Jody. These young women are right; it feels good.

Many of us have held a grudge against our husbands, but Rachel Jones takes the prize for being a champion grudge holder. She and her neighbor, David, had a lovers' quarrel. Every week for forty-two years, David slipped a love letter under Rachel's door in an attempt to mend the quarrel that parted them when both were thirty-two years old. Every letter was burned by the grudge-holding Rachel, and she repeatedly refused to speak to her suitor. Finally, despite the silent treatment, David summoned courage to knock on her door and propose and, to his surprise, she accepted. Both Rachel and David were seventy-four-years old when they finally got married.[1]

What did Rachel gain during her long years of silence? What did she achieve by failing to forgive? She gained loneliness, bitterness, and perhaps a sense of power over another person. Was her vigilant stance of "I'm right, and nothing will make me change my mind!" worth forty-two years of anguish? I wish she were still alive so we could ask her. I strongly suspect, however, that she would tell us that she had been a fool and had wasted years over an issue that mattered very little.

A happy marriage is the union of two good forgivers who commit not to hold a grudge and nurse a hurt, but instead to freely forgive their mate, even though sometimes he or she does not *deserve* forgiveness. This is easy to write, very difficult to accomplish, especially when you are the wounded or misunderstood party. It is difficult, because as Philip Yancey says, "forgiveness is an unnatural act."[2] Yet it is of vital importance, because it is the only way to break the cycle of blame and pain in a relationship. Yancey uses the story of a marriage that disintegrates over a bar of soap as told in the novel *Love in the Time of Cholera* to illustrate what happens when we don't forgive. In the book, it was the wife's job to keep the house in order, including the towels, toilet paper, and soap in the bathroom. One day she forgot to replace the soap, an oversight her husband mentioned in an exaggerated way ("I've been bathing for almost a week without any soap") but that she vigorously denied. Although she had indeed forgotten, her pride was at stake, and she would not back down. What was the outcome of one bar of soap not being in the bathroom? For the next several months, they slept in separate rooms and ate in silence. Author Gabriel Marquez writes that "even when they were old and placid they were careful about bringing it up, for the barely healed wounds could begin to bleed again as if they had been inflicted only yesterday."[3]

How can a bar of soap ruin a marriage? Because neither partner would say, *Stop! This cannot go on. I'm sorry for my part in this. Forgive me.*

Surely we would not be so petty and immature. I wish it weren't so, but I have counseled many women whose marriages were in shambles because they allowed an insignificant incident between husband and wife to blow up into a full-scale civil war—and I, too, have hung on to being "right" over unimportant issues. Over such trivialities, lifelong relationships crack apart, and only forgiveness can halt the widening fissures.

I can shake my head and laugh at a marriage blowing up into a civil war over a bar of soap. I can look at Rachel—holding a grudge for forty-two years—and think, *That is unbelievable.* But do I hold a grudge against my husband for forty-two days? Or forty-two hours? Do you?

What prompts a wife to hold a grudge?

Silly things—words spoken in haste, acts done unknowingly.

Sad things—a forgotten birthday or anniversary, an unkept

promise, a sarcastic slam, or an unpaid bill.

Serious things—rage, vicious words, an emotional affair.

Sordid things—Pornography, adultery, abuse. Physically, emotionally, or sexually harming a child.

When a friend, a colleague, or a family member hurts, misunderstands or wounds you, it is agonizing. But if your partner—chosen for life, the one who knows all your warts and failings—wounds you, the hurt is deeper, the wound more raw. This person is always around; you can't get away from him. You even sleep in the same bed!

I believe the only way you can forgive your intimate companion for silly, sad, serious, and sordid things is to cross over into the supernatural. The natural attitude says, "It is my right to stay mad at you. You deserve it." The supernatural attitude says, "I don't want to stay mad at you. I have forgiven you and reconnected with our love. Life is too short to stay mad." The only way a wife can move into the supernatural is to fall to her knees and cry out to her God, *I can't forgive. Give me the strength and power by the blessed Holy Spirit.*

God is by nature free from the pride and selfishness that by nature is our nature. God forgave us in Christ "while we were yet sinners" (Rom. 5:8)—when we were undeserving, when we turned our backs on Him. God asks us to forgive as He has forgiven us, not once or twice, but as Jesus says, forgive "seventy times seven" (Matt. 18:22). He must have had marriage in mind when He said this, because it is in this most intimate encounter that we are most vulnerable and open to hurt, and where we most often need to forgive.

My friend Dana can tell you about the power of forgiveness. She is an incredible woman who saturates herself in God's Word. She knows God's voice and says yes to God. For several years, she had been in and out of numerous hospitals (including Mayo Clinic and the Stanford Medical Center) for severe health issues. Over ten years of trauma had put deep strain on Dana and Adam's marriage. Adam couldn't see that his words of anger were uncalled for, and Dana waited for him to ask for her forgiveness for a long list of offenses. But he didn't. Soon months had shifted seasons.

Life went on. One evening Adam and Dana even had a date night. She was excited. She had finally gained some weight back after her surgeries. She had a new black dress, and she couldn't wait for Adam to tell her she looked beautiful. But the date turned into a disaster; no words of love, no "You look great!" Adam just wanted to hurry home to get back to work. The next morning Dana decided enough was enough. She stomped toward Adam's office with her list of his offenses. Everything she felt was justified. He was guilty! I'll let Dana tell you what happened:

> With only five steps left before entering the battlefield, I heard a whisper, "Dana, keep your mouth shut. Do not say what you want to say." I knew who it was, and I didn't want to hear. What? Are You kidding me, Lord?
>
> This wasn't the first time God used spiritual duct tape to halt my babble. I knew I needed to obey. The door opened. My husband spun his chair around and said, "Hey, what's up?" All that came out was, "I just came in here to tell you I love you." It was a lie—well not the "I love you" part, because I do love my husband, but it certainly was not the reason I had come to see him. I stood there for a few seconds, not quite believing what had come out of my mouth. He smiled. "I love you, too," he said as I turned around and headed out the door.
>
> What just happened? The tears began to fall. I truly could not remember nine of the ten items that had been stuck in my brain for countless weeks. Okay—the black dress one, I remembered—it was only the night before. But the most amazing thing was that it held no power. My anger was gone. My self-righteousness was gone. My need for him to say, "Please forgive me" was gone. Obeying God— that's all it took—and the reward was a spiritual bath to my soul.

I made it back to my bedroom and prayed, Lord, forgive me. Who am I to throw a punch at my husband? After all we've gone through and all he has sacrificed for me, I should be the one to ask him to forgive me. Would You help me, Lord?

So that night lying side by side, I took Adam's hand. The tears flowed, but so did my overwhelming love for this incredible man God had given to me. The words came easy: "Please forgive me, I'm sorry for ..." Yes the list was long, but it was a list of what I needed to ask forgiveness for: my shortcomings, my quick judgments, the expectations I placed on him that made him feel burdened and defeated. How could I have been so blind? I told him of my great love for him. He, too, asked me to forgive him. God Himself was there: removing the weight of our unforgiving hearts.

I've learned to hear God's voice more clearly now. More often than not, He just whispers the words, "Spiritual duct tape," and I know that obedience is the only choice worth making.

Dana knew what God says about forgiveness in His Word. She listened to His voice, even when she didn't want to hear it. God longs for each of us to make a secret choice to forgive our husband quickly and completely of silly, sad, serious, and sordid things. Yes, staying mad may feel good, and it keeps conviction away, but it robs you and your husband of peace and healing. Think again, my friend. Do you really want to stay mad at your husband?

Insight 2: THREE SHOCKING TRUTHS ABOUT FORGIVENESS

One wife wrote this about why she can't forgive her husband:

I want to stay mad because you are clearly in the wrong and I'm not. If I give up being mad, then it's like I'm lying down and giving up—saying that you're right. I want to stay mad because then I have more ammunition stored up for the day I get to explode. Is this right? No! But it's so hard to let it go and give it up to the Father.

I agree; it is hard to let it go. To encourage you, let me share three shocking truths about forgiveness that have taken me deeper in never wanting to hold a grudge. If you understand them, they will cause you to run to the person who has hurt you and say, "I forgive you."

Hidden in the book of Second Corinthians is the first shocking truth about forgiveness.

1. Forgiving kicks Satan out! The apostle Paul exhorts you and me to forgive quickly and continually. Why? "So that *Satan will not outsmart us. For we are familiar with his evil schemes"* (2 Cor. 2:11 NLT). Outsmarted by Satan? No, thank you! I don't want to be outsmarted by anyone, but I definitely do not want the Deceiver, the Evil One, to outsmart me. Just the thought makes me mad! Do you realize that if you harbor resentment toward your husband, if you refuse to forgive, Satan gets the advantage over you?

Picture your adversary, Satan, squealing with delight because you chose to hold a grudge. He is dancing with glee that he has outsmarted you with his evil schemes. By harboring resentment toward your mate, you open wide a door for Satan. And what will he do? Take advantage of you, manipulate you, trick you, and weasel his wicked lies into your heart. Lies like:

- Why forgive him again, he doesn't deserve it.
- Stay angry, don't walk toward him.
- You'll be a pushover if you forgive him.

What Satan fails to tell you is that if you fail to freely forgive, he wins.

Kick Satan out! Don't let him win!

2. Forgiving invites intimacy with the Lord. You know the Lord's Prayer. Probably you could repeat it right now if asked. So let me ask you, what is the one conditional prayer in the Lord's Prayer? It's not, "Give us this day our daily bread," and not, "Lead us not into temptation." Open your Bible to Matthew 6:9–15 and read these familiar words. Did you see the one prayer that has a condition attached to it? "Forgive us our sins, *as we have forgiven those who sin against us*" (Matt. 6:12 NLT). When you pray this prayer, you ask God to grant you the same kind of forgiveness that you give to your husband. Is this really the kind of forgiveness you want? How free is your forgiveness? Do you hold a husband grudge or forgive freely?

The shocking thing is that God adds a P.S. to the Lord's Prayer. He repeats *only* this conditional prayer about forgiving. He even makes it more explicit. "If you forgive those who sin against you, your heavenly Father will forgive you. But if you refuse to forgive others, your Father will not forgive your sins" (Matt. 6:14–15 NLT). Are you thinking, *Wait a minute, Linda, I thought I was saved by grace through faith. What do you mean God won't forgive me?*

The Lord's Prayer is not about salvation; it is about intimacy and fellowship with the Father. The purpose of the prayer is to show us how to stay in fellowship with God: "If we walk in the Light as He Himself is in the Light, we have fellowship with one another, and the blood of Jesus His Son cleanses us from all sin" (1 John 1:7). R. T. Kendall says, "Walking in the light means following without compromise *anything God shows you to do.* But if He shows you something and you sweep it under the carpet, years later you will wonder why you haven't grown spiritually. The reason will be because you postponed obedience; there was no real fellowship with the Father."[4]

I long for deep intimacy with my Lord. Do you? Then be quick to forgive your husband. Forgiveness places you on the path of deeper fellowship.

3. Forgiving brings glory to you. This third shocking truth about forgiveness is hidden in the book of Proverbs. I have studied and taught the book of Proverbs, and I don't ever remember noticing this important verse:

> *A woman's wisdom gives her patience; it is to her glory to overlook*
> *an offense. (Prov. 19:11, author's paraphrase)*

Stop for a minute and ask yourself, *What would give me honor and glory?*

Getting your dream job?

Receiving the Nobel Peace Prize?

Being "The Mother of the Year"?

Have God tell you, "Well done"?

This verse tucked away in the book of Proverbs says something very different: You receive honor and glory when you forgive freely and overlook an offense.

Amazing.

Renowned Old Testament scholar Dr. Bruce Waltke says the glory a woman receives when she forgives the sin of another is like an "attractive adornment [she] wears." When a wife forgives, "people delight and rejoice in [her] and [she] wins … more fame, honor, praise, and distinction" through forgiving than in any other way.[5]

The adornment a forgiving wife wears is a sweet fragrance that reminds others of the Lord Jesus. Her calm and gentle spirit, her tender smile, radiates peace and joy because forgiveness has set her free from resentment and anger. I long to be clothed with this adornment.

My friend Katie already wears it. Eleven years ago, her world exploded without warning. The family she worked so hard to build and maintain was destroyed. It began with a phone call from the Children's Advocacy Center, asking her to come to the center about a matter involving her oldest daughter, Hannah. Once there, Katie received the worst news of her life. Hannah was accusing her father, Katie's husband, of sexually molesting her.

Katie called me to come to pray with her. The anguish was indescribable for her and for both her daughters. She says, "That first day I didn't know if I would even stay married to Craig, or what my future would look like, but I did know that I would have to cling to God and trust Him in a deeper way than I ever had before."

Craig was arrested, pled guilty, and was later sentenced to a halfway house for ninety days. Additionally, he was given probation for five years, which included attending weekly counseling and a group therapy program for sexual offenders. This sentence meant Craig could not come home for several years. Because he repented and immediately went to their pastor to confess, Katie believed she needed to be willing to walk toward him with forgiveness. Psalm 51:12 became her prayer: *Father, grant me a willing spirit!*

I'll let her tell you how God answered her prayer.

I learned a lot about forgiveness watching Hannah. It took her two years of sobbing, screaming, and fighting before she could give up her anger and say from the heart, "I forgive you, Dad." I was still struggling. I was trying to forgive, but the shock of my husband's betrayal was so great, and my trust so destroyed, it took seeing my own sin before I could take the necessary steps to forgive Craig. God showed me many things during my journey to forgiveness, but these three stand out in my memory:

First, I had to "get the log out of my own eye" (Matt. 7:3–5) in order to see my own sin and how I had pushed my husband away from intimacy. God showed me in Romans 2:11 that He does not have favorites. He wanted my healing, but He wanted Craig's healing too. How could I want God to forgive me and yet punish him?

Second, I learned firsthand that God's ways are above our ways (Isa. 55:9). He called me to repair the breach in this relationship, even though I was not the one who blew a big hole in the wall. God stripped everything away that was important to me and put me in a place where I was utterly dependent on Him.

Third, I committed to doing whatever I could to be a blessing to my husband (1 Peter 3:8–18). How many ways are there to do this? I truly did find countless ways to bless my husband, starting with "a soft word turns away wrath."

As I sought to give a blessing to Craig, God blessed me and my family. Many thought this betrayal was too hard to repair. Craig and I lived apart for over five years, and during that time he received counseling and demonstrated to me, our family, and to his counselor that he was truly on the road to healing, so I felt it was safe to invite him back into our home. Eleven long years later, I stand in awe of my God who is the Healer and the One who can heal anything! I'm moved to tears as I compile this list of God's many blessings on our family:

- *My marriage is completely restored and flourishing in all areas.*
- *My daughter is completely reconciled to her father, and she even asked him to walk her down the aisle at her wedding!*
- *Both our daughters are happily married, and my husband is a father to our young sons-in-law.*
- *Our family all attend church together.*
- *My husband and I have served our church by leading financial workshops and now teach a marriage Bible study for couples.*
- *I have had the privilege of walking with many women who are suffering betrayal by their husbands.*
- *We are completely debt-free after years of financial hardship, job loss, legal and medical expenses. God has blessed us beyond our wildest dreams.*

- *God has given us a heart for others, and we now comfort others with the same comfort with which we were comforted.*
- *AND this man who betrayed his whole family is today the beloved grandpa of Hannah's new daughter!*

God is so glorified, but let me tell you, I've never seen a woman in the agony Katie lived in for years. She made heart-wrenching choices daily. I remember her saying to me, "Linda, if I have to be in this pain, I hope God will make me into a gracious woman." I wish you could know Katie and see the peace and joy that radiates from her smile. Truly, her family is a walking miracle. And Katie is a gracious woman, all because she chose to forgive.

Not every husband is willing to repent and go through five long years of restoration and healing before being allowed to go back home. Craig is a man I call friend and deeply respect. He is proof that even in the most horrible of situations, when forgiveness is given and received, God can heal.

Insight 3: STRIP OFF ANGER, PUT ON FORGIVENESS

As I talk to women about their thoughts on forgiving, I see a new idea of forgiveness roaming around in hearts: Forgiveness is conditional. It comes across in comments like this:

- "My husband doesn't deserve forgiveness."
- "I don't think he is really sorry."
- "Look at the pain he's caused me—why should I let him off the hook?"
- "What he did was wrong!"
- "I'm always the one to forgive; it's his turn."

Let's return to Paul's statement in Ephesians 4:31–32. These are my all-time favorite verses on forgiveness. And they are very clear: We are commanded to strip off our anger and put on forgiveness.

Strip off! "Let all bitterness and wrath and anger and clamor and slander be put away from you, along with all malice." (Eph. 4:31)

Put on! "Be kind to one another, tender-hearted, forgiving each other, just as God in Christ also has forgiven you." (Eph. 4:32)

We are to strip off our old, harmful ways of relating. These six attitudes are to be tossed in the trash bin:

1. Bitterness. Nursing your wrath to keep it warm—brooding over insults, injuries, and slights that you've received. Aristotle spoke of bitterness as "the resentful spirit which refuses reconciliation."

2. Wrath. The flaring up of passion and temper, an outbreak of anger that springs from personal animosity.

3. Anger. A long-lived habitual anger, where it settles down and is at home in your heart.

4. Clamor. The loud self-assertion of an angry wife who wants everyone to hear her grievances.

5. Evil speaking. Slanderous or abusive speaking about one's husband.

6. Malice. Bad feelings of every kind that cause a wife to speak or do evil against her husband.

Bitterness, wrath, anger, clamor, evil speaking, and malice: six negative attitudes that we must strip off. Declare, "No more anger and slander for me!" Strip yourselves of your old selfish, angry ways of relating. Build a bonfire, and banish them forever!

Instead, put on a new wardrobe. Its shades of kindness, compassion, and forgiveness make your skin glow—your eyes sparkle.

The vibrant, yet soft, colors of your new garments are amazing.

1. Kindness. This is love in practical action. When you put on kindness, you are as concerned about your husband's feelings as you are about your own. You are as sensitive to your husband's sorrows, hurts, and struggles as to your own.

2. *Tenderheartedness.* The love in action that is kindness must be married to a tender heart of sympathy. The obstacle to kindness and compassion is often the sense of wrong done to you as a wife or a grievance nursed. So the overarching garment you must put on is forgiveness.

3. *Forgiveness.* The Greek word *charizoma,* translated as forgiving, means "to be gracious" or "to give freely."[6] The idea as expressed in *The Amplified Bible* is "forgiving one another [readily and freely], as God in Christ forgave you" (Eph. 4:32).

I love the way *The Message* describes your new wardrobe: "Be gentle with one another, sensitive. Forgive one another as quickly and thoroughly as God in Christ forgave you."

Colette had an agonizing decision to make about stripping off the old and putting on the new. After twenty-five years of marriage, she discovered her husband was very different from the man she had loved and trusted. As I was writing this book, I gave Colette the first Dangerous Question and encouraged her to write her Marriage Purpose Statement. She threw the manuscript in the trash. But God worked in her heart, and three months later Colette was ready to think about her marriage. She desperately needed God's wisdom, and He spoke to her from Exodus 34:1, where God told Moses He would rewrite His words on new tablets, replacing the tablets that had been shattered. Colette did not know if new words could ever be written, replacing the fragmented vows of her marriage, but God then spoke to her again, saying, "Trust Me."

She chose to obey, but she could commit to her marriage goals for only three months, and no longer. This is what she wrote:

I ask You, Jesus, to write on my heart new words that I can commit to. I cannot even begin to project a lifetime marriage statement, though my face is resolutely set towards a long obedience to my God, therefore to my husband. But I can commit to three months of purposeful, prayed over, "I wills."

- *I will forgive, and I will ask for forgiveness, purposefully and prayerfully each day. "As far as the east is from the west" I will not bring up forgiven hurts again. In my forgiving, I will release my husband of his "debts" so that he may walk in freedom and grow towards Light.*
- *I will relinquish all judging, self-righteous attitudes and my prideful heart. God alone is the righteous and holy Judge. It is not my job.*
- *I will be present in body and spirit to my husband, actively engaging with his needs. I will not manipulate him with absence of spirit, lack of attention, or withdrawal.*
- *I will be respectful, accepting his leadership.*
- *I will not dwell on the darkness in him, nor fear it. Rather, I will live out Philippians 4:8: Whatever is true, whatever is honorable, whatever is right, pure, lovely, whatever is of good repute, in my husband, excellent, worthy of praise, these are what I will discipline my mind to dwell on.*
- *I will be merciful to my husband, remembering the truth that my Father's mercies are new to us every morning.*
- *I will recognize, and celebrate, each decision for Life and Light my husband makes.*
- *I will not give up hope, for my hope is in God Himself, who is caring for me and protecting me.*

These things, my Lord, I commit to You, fully understanding that it is only through Your Holy Spirit and by Your incredible grace to me that I can even pen these words. May You be praised!

If you think the words Colette wrote flowed easily, you've never been in gut-wrenching pain. As I write, I can see her eyes; they overflow with sorrow. In her grief, this woman of faith stripped off her old clothes and put on her beautiful new wardrobe of kindness, compassion, and forgiveness.

Do you remember that Colette said she could not imagine committing to her "I wills" for a lifetime? Five months after writing her three-month Marriage Purpose Statement, she wrote: "May 15, 2010. Today I declare that this Marriage Purpose Statement is till death do us part."

P.S. Five months after Collette added "till death do us part" to her Marriage Purpose Statement, I received the following email from her.

> *God is beyond good! I'm not sure about the when, Linda, but my husband and I are in relationship again. I don't think I really thought this could ever happen…. God's exact kind of situation to His Glory! I big miss my husband when he's out of town…. I wait for him to come home at night with expectancy. I want to care for him again and spend time just because. And I am looking forward to a life together. CAN YOU BELIEVE IT?*

Who says God doesn't do miracles today? Collette's story qualifies as a miracle. I know. I watched it happen!

Insight 4: ANOINT WITH FORGIVENESS

Many women in my survey felt that offering the gift of forgiveness was the best thing they did for their marriage.

> *I decided to live in forgiveness. (Married forty years)*

> *FORGIVE! I forgave him for his affair, and God has restored our marriage! (Married twenty-three years)*

Six years ago, my husband confessed and repented of his infidelity to me of eleven years. At that point I had a choice to make—anger and bitterness or forgiveness. The BEST decision I made was to begin the process of forgiveness and restoration in my marriage. (Married thirty-seven years)

I learned to say, "I'm sorry." And this is RECENT! (Married twenty-four years)

I chose to forgive and let God restore our marriage, bringing beauty from ashes. (Married twenty-five years)

Learning to be the first to say "I'm sorry." (Married twelve years)

I forgave my husband, not only for the decisions he made that damaged our marriage, I forgave him for everything. (Married thirty years)

Thirty-one years ago he had an affair. The best thing I ever did was forgive him and begin changing my life. I chose to not look at his wrong but at my own problems. (Married thirty-five years)

Several of these wives forgave their husbands for sexual sins. All sin is difficult to forgive, but a husband's sexual sin touches a wife at the core of her being. There is a unique knowing when a wife opens herself up to her husband during sexual intercourse. She opens her soul, her body, and her emotions. Discovering her husband has "known" another woman pierces her in the core of her being. Connie knew this deep piercing.

She tried to forgive, but when the images came again and again, she wondered if she really had. She wanted out of the roller-coaster ride of questioning whether she had really forgiven him. To move forward, Connie decided to cement in her mind that she had made the choice to forgive by acting out her forgiveness in a beautiful way. Here is what happened:

> *I was shaking as I asked my husband to stand in front of me. I took off all of his clothes, and with a bottle of scented oil, I anointed his body.*
>
> *I touched his forehead: "I forgive your mind for thinking thoughts of her."*
>
> *I touched his ears: "I forgive your ears for listening to her."*
>
> *I touched his hands: "I forgive your hands for touching her."*
>
> *After anointing every part of his body, I came to his feet: "I forgive your feet for walking toward her." As the words came, tears cascaded down my face. Relief flooded me. The past was truly in the past—for both of us.*[7]

Sheryl heard me tell Connie's story of the Forgiveness Anointing at a conference. She wept bitter tears because she knew she could not be like Connie. Sheryl wrote me the following email:

> *In the immediate aftermath of learning that my husband had become sexually intimate with another, I allowed anger and unforgiveness to choke out the love of so many years. I surrendered to the pain, and I held him in contempt. Though he begged me to forgive him, I could not. So he walked away. Connie's story caused me to weep for what I had lost.*
>
> *My husband has moved and begun a new life, a life he has no desire to make me a part of. Still, I knew what I had to do. I called him and asked for a few minutes of his time. I traveled to his city and met him in a church. I had the CD of you sharing Connie's story and played it for my husband. I wept again and told him, "I'm sorry I could not be that woman. I'm sorry I didn't know how*

to forgive you sooner." I asked him if he would allow me to express my forgiveness in a similar physical act (except the "take off your clothes" part). He said yes.

Sitting beneath a tree, outside the church with anointing oil in hand, I touched my husband's eyes, his ears, his hands, his feet, and his heart. Through almost choking sobs, I managed to speak the words and give him the forgiveness he had begged me for so long ago. When I opened my eyes, this ever-strong man had tears tumbling down both cheeks. For a moment, neither of us spoke. Finally, I thanked him for forgiving ME, forgiving me for not being the woman I should have been when he came to me to repent of his sin. He then thanked me for forgiving him for not loving me and remaining faithful to our vows.

If only I could have done this sooner.

If only that moment would not have ended with us climbing into separate cars to return to our now-separate lives.

If only … words of regret, words of sorrow, for what might have been. I weep over Sheryl's loss.

Whatever barrier is between you and your husband, don't wait until it is too late. Don't let "If only I could have done this sooner" be your story. Forgiving is wrenching; it costs us. But not forgiving costs more. God commands us to forgive freely as we have been forgiven in Christ. There are blessings bestowed on the one who forgives. Today is the day to offer forgiveness!

Insight 5: BE A PROACTIVE FORGIVER

Think back to the last time you were blistering mad at your husband. Never heard *blistering* and *mad* together? It is when hot sparks of anger are erupting out of every cell in your body. If you've been there, you know what it is. This is not a time to consider forgiveness. Oh, you should consider it, but you can't. You're too spitfire indignant that your husband could be so dense, inconsiderate, irresponsible, inept, immoral, disgusting, _____ (you fill in the blank).

In the heat of the moment, forgiveness is the last thing you want to do. That is why I encourage you to make the decision to forgive *before* you need to forgive. You must be proactive about offering forgiveness for big things and for daily little things. Forgiveness is one of the most difficult parts of marriage and also one of the most important. So go before the Lord and pour out your heart NOW. Decide NOW to be a proactive forgiver!

Once you have made this secret choice, how do you forgive? What practical, physical symbol will substantiate to your mind and heart that you have forgiven?

Here are some ideas to consider:

1. Let your fingers do your forgiving. Consider the following story about Winston Churchill.

> *At a dinner party one night Lady Churchill was seated across the table from Sir Winston, who kept making his hand walk up and down—two fingers bent at the knuckles. The fingers appeared to be walking toward Lady Churchill. Finally, her dinner partner asked, "Why is Sir Winston looking at you so wistfully, and whatever is he doing with those two knuckles on the table?" "That's simple," she replied. "We had a mild quarrel before we left home, and he is indicating it's his fault and he's on his knees to me in abject apology."[8]*

2. Put "ISSUMAGJOUJUNGNAINERMIK" on your refrigerator. When missionaries first went to the Eskimos, they could not find a word in their language for forgiveness, so they had to compound one. This turned out to be ISSUMAGJOUJUNGNAINERMIK. It is a formidable looking group of letters that has a beautiful meaning for those who understand it. It means "Not-being-able-to-think-about-it-anymore."[9]

I have ISSUMAGJOUJUNGNAINERMIK posted in large letters on my refrigerator. I get some strange looks when people see it, but it reminds me to forgive freely, to not think about it anymore.

3. Let the leaves flutter away your offense. When I feel my body and soul holding resentment against my husband, I take a walk alone. I pick up leaves and hold them tightly in my closed hand. Then I pray, something like this: *My Father, You see my heart. You know I've clutched on to resentment toward Jody for how he's treated me. I'm opening my hand, Lord, and watching the leaves fall through my fingers. I give it up; I let go of holding on to the offense.*

4. Throw the rock of bitterness away. When I sense my heart is holding on to bitterness and anger, I go outside and find a quiet place alone, fall to my knees and tell my Father what He already knows: *Forgive me for hanging on in my heart. I'm throwing off the anger and bitter feelings toward Jody.* I pick up a rock, name it Bitterness, throw it as far as I can throw, and tell God I am banishing bitterness.

5. *Exchange your anger with prayer.* Stormie Omartian says, "Something amazing happens to your heart when you pray for another person. The hardness melts. You become able to get beyond the hurts, and forgive. It's miraculous! It happens because when we pray, we enter into the presence of God and He fills us with His Spirit of love. When you pray for your husband, the love of God will grow in your heart for him."[10]

I thank my Lord and Savior that He didn't look at me and evaluate whether I deserved forgiveness. What if He had said:

Linda doesn't deserve it.

I don't think she is really sorry.

Look at the pain Linda's caused Me. Why should I let her

off the hook?

What Linda did was wrong.

I'm always the One to forgive; it's Linda's turn.

Jesus' example humbles me and encourages me to follow in His steps. The beauty and glory of Christ's forgiveness is that it is unconditional. He paid the price for my sin, and I just say, "Thank You!" It is glorious to receive God's forgiveness, but then He turns to me and says, "Now, Linda, you extend forgiveness to Jody, the same unconditional forgiveness I've given you—and, Linda, remember to do it with kindness and compassion."

Dangerous Prayer!

Lord, I see why I want to stay mad at my husband. Teach me to be tenderhearted and forgiving toward him, just as God in Christ has forgiven me.

Is It Possible to Grow Together When Things Fall Apart?

My eyes are fixed on you, O Sovereign LORD; in you I take refuge.
Psalm 141:8 (NIV)

*You will keep in perfect peace all who trust in
you, all whose thoughts are fixed on you!*
Isaiah 26:3 (NLT)

I always view problems as opportunities in work clothes.
Henry Kaiser

*It doesn't matter ... how great the pressure is.
It only matters where the pressure lies.*
Hudson Taylor

Insight 1: AN ANNIVERSARY ON THE BLUE DANUBE
1991—Home was in Vienna, Austria. With three kids in college that year
and four the year before, our cupboards were beyond bare, and a camping

trip was the most I could expect for an anniversary celebration. What a wonderful surprise when our travel agent gave us two nights at the Budapest Hilton plus one three-course meal. I liked camping, but an anniversary atop the walled part of old Budapest overlooking the Danube and picturesque Parliament building definitely won over the old rusty camper in the romance department.

Visions of a candlelight dinner at a Hungarian restaurant, strolling musicians, and a view of incredible beauty filled my thoughts. I was ready for this. Jody and I had gone camping on our honeymoon. The Budapest Hilton overlooking the Danube was definitely a step up, and I liked the step.

The view *was* breathtaking, the Castle, Museum, Fishermen's Bastion, and Matthias Church, all amazing and otherworldly. The food and music was all I'd anticipated, the moonlight walk overlooking the river, breathtakingly romantic. Everything was just right, all the physical circumstances in place. There was romance, but the romance reflected the sadness of the romancers.

At one point Jody said, "I'm sorry this weekend has to be like this." When the anniversary getaway was planned, no one knew his father would have just died, that our future would be one big question mark. Amid the Old World beauty, we were experiencing one of the most difficult times of our life together. Not exactly an atmosphere conducive to an anniversary celebration. But as we drove home to Vienna, I told this man I'd loved for almost thirty years that I'd never felt closer to him than now. We had wept together, talked and prayed, been silent together, and shared an intimacy that goes beyond words.

What creates intimacy? Of course fun, laughter, intimate sharing, and abandoned sex do. But deep emotional bonding is also found in the hard times—when we cry, when answers evade us, when God seems far away, but we cling to Him and to each other. How glorious it would be if marriage were all picnics, parties, and glorious lovemaking. No pain, no problems, no perplexing circumstances. Yes, we could definitely get used to that. But it is not to be, not for me or for you. If it isn't already, crisis will be a part of your marriage.

Crises come wrapped in packages of all shapes and sizes. There are little boxes, in-between-size boxes, gigantic boxes, and boxes labeled personal crisis, couple crisis, kid crisis, job crisis, home crisis, everyday crisis, sexual crisis, health crisis, life crisis. Webster defines *crisis* as "a situation that has reached a critical phase; an unstable or crucial time."[1]

In a marriage, a crisis presents the potential for:

> *Danger that the crisis will tear us apart and destroy our oneness.*

> *Opportunity that the crisis will push us together and deepen our oneness.*

Since crisis will be part of your life and marriage, how do you turn it into an opportunity to grow closer to your husband?

1. *Know God's viewpoint.* Knowing God's perspective will enable you to not just survive but thrive in times of crisis. No place in Scripture are we promised a problem-free life—or marriage. In fact, Jesus said just the opposite: "Here on earth you will have many trials and sorrow. But take heart, because I have overcome the world" (John 16:33 NLT).

Mariah did not know God's viewpoint, and she listened to friends, not God. She shared her view with me at a conference.

> *I just don't get it. Marriage wasn't supposed to be this hard. I prayed about who to marry, we're Christians ... but every area of our marriage is a challenge: our finances, communication (we don't talk, we nag, sneer, and shout at each other), and sex. Don't even mention sex. My friend said that if you are really pleasing God that you won't have all the problems we're having.*

If the friend is right, Jody and I must not be pleasing God, because our marriage has been filled with trials. The friend has wrong thinking. Some Christians believe that if you're walking with the Lord, you will be delivered *from* trouble. But the promise of God is deliverance *in times of* trouble, which is quite different. God says there will be trials and sorrows. The blessing is, we have the Problem-Solver living within. He is our peace in the midst of panic and pain. But panic and pain *will come,* because crisis is no respecter of persons. Couples who love Christ and follow Him have deep trials. Couples who claim no God have deep trials.

2. Apply God's Word to the crisis. God's Word makes some unbelievable statements about how we are to respond in trials. One is found in James 1:2: We are to count it joy when we encounter trials.

Really? Did James really mean I was to say, "This is joy to us," when it feels like our world is falling apart in the midst of a romantic anniversary trip? I'm to count it joy when I feel grief over the death of Jody's father and complete confusion about our future?

A look at other translations and paraphrases confirms that this is indeed the meaning behind the Greek text:

> *Consider it all joy, my [sisters], when you encounter various trials.*

> *Consider it a sheer gift, friends, when tests and challenges come at you from all sides.* (MSG)

> *When all kinds of trials and temptations crowd into your lives, my [sisters], don't resent them as intruders, but welcome them as friends!* (PH)

All joy? A sheer gift? Pain as a friend? If you are like me, trials feel like intruders, not friends. Pain isn't the gift I want. Joy would be having the floods, fires, earthquakes, sexual pain, cancer, abuse, uncertainty—having *all* pain—*leave,* and the quicker the better. If we're honest, we don't welcome pain as a friend. We say: *"Get away from me! I don't want the process to go on. I hate distress, I hate tension. I just want it over."* In fact, I think most women count it all joy when they *escape* trials.

James said to count it all joy *in the midst* of trials. And there is a reason. Believe it or not, God says there are benefits to trials. Look with me at the next verses.

> *Consider it all joy … when you encounter various trials, knowing that the testing of your faith produces endurance. And let endurance have its perfect result, so that you may be perfect and complete, lacking nothing. (James 1:2–4)*

We are promised the benefit of endurance when we encounter a crisis. If we meet the testing in the right way, we will become stable, and our character will look more like Christ's character.

Looking like Christ is definitely a benefit!

James' message is this: Trials can be faced with joy because, if joy is infused with faith, endurance results—and if endurance goes full-term, it will develop a thoroughly mature Christian who lacks nothing. You will indeed be all God wants you to be.

So think on this. When a trial comes, you have a choice:

You can clench your fist and fight God. If this is your choice, you will become angry, griping, and bitter. Or …

You can open your hands and say, *God, this trial is very difficult. It feels unfair. But I want to trust You in it. Please work endurance in me. I want to become like Christ.*

As individuals and as marriage partners, we are to rejoice in the difficult things God allows in our life and relationship. I paraphrase James 1:2–4 like this for my marriage:

Rejoice in the trials you face as a couple; they will teach you per-severance and make your love and commitment to one another strong. They will produce character, a strength that will lead to intimacy.

I will always remember the anniversary trip, not because of the beautiful Danube River but because of the closeness Jody and I experienced amid the pain. Yes, it is possible to grow closer during crisis!

Insight 2: TRUSTING GOD WHEN LIFE HURTS

2010—Living in Monument, Colorado. In times of trial, God's perspective is what we need most, yet our hearts and minds focus on what we can see and touch. When what we are seeing goes from minor crisis to major crisis, we get stuck in our own perspective. Rather than waiting on our Lord to solve our dilemma in His own time, we want to step in and manipulate a fast, painless escape.

When we are faced with a trial, we prefer a tangible way out to God's telling us to trust Him to see us through. It is easier to escape with your husband and put a moratorium on the problem—and even easier to try to take control than it is to trust. Trusting God during a crisis is difficult, because we don't know how long the crisis will continue or what the outcome will be. We don't know how long we will have to trust. Trust is the answer to worry, but when your child has cancer, your business is bankrupt, or your beloved is deeply depressed, the logical perspective is to worry.

This week, while editing this chapter, one phone call from a doctor restructured our lives. Jody has cancer, and surgery is scheduled. The questions for Jody and me are:

Will the crisis of cancer tear us apart and destroy our oneness?

Or …

Will the crisis of cancer push us closer together and deepen our oneness?

And God has a personal question for me as a wife. *Linda, will you worry or trust?* So I turn once again to a much-loved passage of Scripture, and pray, *Lord, teach me in a fresh and new way how to trust You.*

In Proverbs 3:5–6, I am told how to trust in a practical way, what my part is in trusting and what God's part is. I have this passage glued to the crevices of my mind because it has been such an encouragement to me in times of crisis. And I need it today.

> *Trust in the LORD with all your heart and do not lean on your own understanding. In all your ways acknowledge Him and He will make your paths straight.*

Ask God to open your spiritual eyes to see this familiar passage in a new and deeper way. I see four verbs: Three are directed at me, one toward God. My part is to "trust," "lean not," and "acknowledge," and God's part is "to make my paths straight." One little word is mentioned four times in these two verses: the word *your.* Your responsibility in a crisis situation is to:

> *Trust with all YOUR heart*
> *Refuse to lean on YOUR understanding,*
> *Acknowledge Him in all YOUR ways,*
> *So that He might make straight YOUR paths.*

What do these four *yours* mean to me?

First, "Trust with all your heart." For me this means that I express my trust in God by thanking Him for what He will do in this crisis. I am asked to "give thanks in all circumstances" (1 Thess. 5:18 NIV), so in my current circumstances I am telling the Lord:

> *My Father, this situation makes no sense to me. I don't understand it, but I thank You for what You are going to accomplish because*

*of it. By thanking You, I'm saying to You, I trust You to know bet-
ter than I know. I trust You even though I can't see what You are
doing. In Romans 5:3–5 You promise that the results of trusting
You in this situation are character, perseverance, and hope.*

Second, "Lean not on your own understanding." I talk to myself:
"Linda, stay away from trying to figure it out. Throw out your own ideas
to fix it. Toss your creative manipulation in the trash." And then I pray,
*Lord, instead of leaning on my clever plan to fix the mess, I want to lean, as on
a crutch, on You, my Father God.*

I will rest the full weight of my problem on God—all the pressure off
of me and transferred onto Him.

Third, "In all your ways acknowledge Him." To *acknowledge* means "to
recognize." Rather than leaning on my finite understanding, I acknowledge
that God is the Blessed Controller of all things, even Jody's cancer. *Lord,
I bow and worship You. You are the Blessed Controller of all things. I declare
this is true.*

Fourth, "God will make your paths straight." The Hebrew word for
straight means "to make smooth, straight, right, and includes the idea of
removing obstacles that are in the way."[2] God says His part is to straighten
the stressful paths. He doesn't say when or how; He just promises He will.
So I thank Him: *My God, thank You that in Your infinite wisdom You see how
to make smooth this stressful path. I praise You.*

We need to practice trusting; we need to practice leaning; we need to
practice acknowledging—and we need to practice these things in times
of anxiety, in times of peace, in times of crisis, in times of joy. If we
wait until the crisis hits, we'll worry instead of trust. Our finite human
perspective will take front seat because it's more natural to us than God's
eternal perspective. Join me in memorizing Proverbs 3:5–6, and trust,
lean not, and acknowledge Him, knowing that He will straighten out
our paths.

The promise in these verses is wonderful. When I understand in my mind and heart what these passion-filled words in Proverbs 3:5–6 mean, then I can personalize them as a prayer to my Father God for help:

> *I will throw myself completely upon You, my Lord. I will cast all my present and future needs on You because You are my intimate Savior-God. I find in only You my true security and safety. I will do this with all my mind and feeling and will. I know I must refuse to support myself upon the crutch of my clever ingenuity. Instead, I recognize Your presence and concern for every minute detail of my problem. I know You will take full control of all that concerns me; You will remove all the rocks along the way and will smooth out and make straight my paths. Thank You, Abba, Father![8]*

Jody and I have made our choice: The crisis of cancer is not going to pull us apart. We will trust Him in the crisis and cling to each other as we face this crisis together.

Insight 3: MARRIAGE CRISIS!

I want to introduce you to two special women who would tell you that even in a very difficult marriage crisis, it is possible for a couple to grow closer together. Both women have walked the hard road of abuse by their husband: Tabitha suffered the pain of pornography; Corina endured the pain of verbal abuse. Here are their stories:

Tabi's story. While Peter and Tabitha were dating, she discovered a stack of *Playboy* magazines in his closet. She thought they were gross and told him to toss them in the trash. Peter did as Tabi asked and threw the magazines away, but he admits that he thought she was overreacting. He didn't see any harm in porn. His parents took a picture of him looking at a *Playboy* when he was a boy of seven, and he'd been raised to think looking at porn was part of what it means to be a man. As Peter tossed the magazines in the trash can, Tabi thought, *Good riddance.* She had no idea how pornography affected a man's mind. She didn't know it changes a man's heart from who he wants to be to a man enslaved. She didn't know that pornography brings pain to more marriages than anyone can imagine.[4] And she didn't know that Peter continued to look at porn secretly.

Tabi had her own issues to deal with—a date rape in college. Because she was given the date rape drug, she remembered little of the sexual encounter. Though it left deep wounds in her heart, she thought if she couldn't remember it, she could pretend it didn't happen. Tabi had told Peter she was a virgin, but as she grew as a Christian, she realized she should have told him the truth, so two children and ten years into their marriage, she asked him to forgive her for not being honest. Peter couldn't have been sweeter or more understanding. He grieved for her pain.

Tabi sent me an email, telling me how her honesty brought about new oneness.

> *My honesty propelled us to study the Song of Solomon, and we did that with* Intimacy Ignited.[5] *When we got to the part about giving your body to your spouse as a gift, Peter read to me that for a man giving his body was to give his eyes. He was to commit to look only at his wife's body. I wasn't prepared for what happened next. He began sobbing and fell to his knees by the side of the bed. Out poured his continued addiction to porn. What really hurt were these words, "Sometimes when I'm with you, my mind is someplace else."*
>
> *I was so broken, so wounded. I didn't want to deal with this. I wanted to walk away and say, "I'm done! All men are disgusting!"*
>
> *Instead, I prayed and asked God to do something (like heal my husband now!). But God had something very different in mind. He said, "Tabi, make a commitment to never again refuse your husband sexually. Be totally available." Was God kidding? I*

thought this was very unfair and asked God, "Why did I have to do all the giving?" I was the one hurt here. Yet, every time I had my quiet time and was in the Word of God, He would whisper, "Make a commitment to never again refuse your husband sexually. Be totally available."

Finally I said yes to God. I was sure now He would pat me on the back and say, "Good job, Tabi, I'm really proud of you." Again God's response surprised me. "Tell Peter." "What? You can't be serious, God!" When I told Peter, he shouted, "YES!" I was amazed at what my gift did for him. And for me? It released me. I was no longer imprisoned by my past, always asking, "Do I want to do this tonight?" It freed me to give, and that freedom was so amazing. I was finally free to communicate during sex, to say what pleased me. By following God's personally tailored plan, I went from believing sex was a "necessary evil" in marriage to embracing God's beautiful gift of the one-flesh union.

Recently a couple we didn't know asked us if we were newlyweds. We laughed and said, "No." "Well, the way you look at each other, the way you are with each other made us think that."

Praise God for Tabi and Peter's renewed body, soul, and spirit intimacy. This wife chose to seek and obey God rather than allow her marriage crisis, while very painful and daunting, to come between her and her husband. This husband repented and sought help for his addiction. Tabi says, "The crisis of porn brought us even closer together. And I am so proud of my husband. He covenanted with God to give his eyes only to me—and that is what he is doing. At work recently, while waiting for a long download on the computer, the guys wanted to put on nude movies. Peter took the lead and said, 'We're not doing that. No nudity.'"

Corina's story. Corina came to me in tears after an *Intimate Issues* workshop and shared that she had suffered through years of verbal abuse from her husband, James. In his most recent verbal attack, he told her that he didn't find her attractive and that she needed to take better care of herself. (All I can say is, I wish I looked like Corina.) James didn't like anything she did. I cried with Corina and prayed for her. I had no answers but encouraged her to trust God and ask Him to show her what to do, and that is what she did. I'll let her tell you what God led her to do in her personal crisis.

After the retreat, I purchased Intimate Issues *and read it. Not all of it related to me, but God taught me some new things about me and some creative ways to communicate with my husband....*
I realized James wouldn't berate me if he felt connected to me. How can you put down someone you are intimately connected to? So, I tried it in various ways. God showed me to not just ask him, "How was your day?" but to ask specific questions and try to connect with him. Well, it worked. He opened up and we started dialoguing daily, and our communication improved and the way he talked to me improved.

Eleven weeks ago, he left for six months [he's in the military]. Right after he left, he started a new relationship with Jesus Christ. He is Spirit-filled and Spirit-led and has a completely new relationship with God. He was adamant that I come visit him for a very short trip for our eleventh anniversary (even though I had to jump through hoops to get childcare, tickets, work covered, etc.). But I did it, and James surprised me with so many sweet and romantic things! Best of all—he wrote out for me (and read at dinner) 101 reasons why he loves me. It is my most treasured gift from him.

The weekend was the best time of our marriage. He is a truly different person. I didn't demand for him to find God or to study the Bible. He came to it on his own and has stepped up to the plate as the spiritual leader of our home.

I wish I could include all the 101 reasons James gave for why he loves Corina, but there isn't space here, so fifteen reasons will have to do. James really thought about these reasons….

1. I love you because you truly are my best friend.

2. I love when you cross your leg over mine in bed.

3. I love you because you make me feel like a man.

4. I love you because you trust me with your body when we make love.

5. I love you because your hand fits just right in mine.

6. I love you because you have forgiven me.

7. I love you because you have always been the rock and foundation of our marriage and family.

8. I love you because you believe in the power of prayer.

9. I love you because you believe in me.

10. I love you because you always encourage me.

11. I love you because you never gave up on us.

12. I love you because you snort when I make you laugh.

13. I love you because you know how to touch me just right.

14. I love you because you have taught me what it means to truly experience love.

15. I love knowing that I will see you in heaven, and if I died today, my life was better because you loved me.

WOW! Truly what happened in Corina and James' marriage is as much a miracle as if God had healed them from a terminal illness. Their marriage was terminal, and God intervened.

Instead of walking away in anger or shutting their husbands out, both Tabi and Corina trusted God with their marriage crisis and asked Him to intervene and work in their hearts and in their husbands' hearts. God used a wife's loving perseverance to push Corina and James closer together. Through the crisis of pornography, God brought Tabitha and Peter closer together.

Are you facing a crisis in your marriage? God longs to show you how He can give you His peace in the midst of pain and crisis. Call out to Him, cast all your worry and anxiety on Him, and He promises to hold you and your problem. "You can throw the whole weight of your anxiety on Him for you are His personal concern" (1 Peter 5:7 PH).

The Amplified Bible says it like this:

> *Casting the whole of your care [all your anxieties, all your worries, all your concerns, once and for all] on Him, for He cares for you affectionately and cares about you watchfully.*

Today as your heart aches because crisis mode hurts, cling to the promise that your personal Father is caring affectionately about you, your husband, and your marriage. He loves you. While you sleep tonight, He will be watching through the night, carrying all that concerns you on His strong shoulders. He is your peace in times of crisis. He gives the strength you and your husband need to grow closer, even in times of crisis.

Insight 4: A LONG, DIFFICULT MARRIAGE

When Natalie and Paul married, they had planned to serve the Lord together, but this was not to be. Paul became very disillusioned by the sexual sin and double lives of ministry coworkers, and as a result, he has not been to church in fifteen years.

I asked Natalie to describe what her marriage to Paul is like, and this is what she said:

- Paul is not unlovable, but he is sometimes very difficult to love.
- Paul is harsh. I am convinced that my husband's heart is kind and good, but sometimes his expression is not. It hurts.
- Paul did several things that broke our vows and my trust in a major way. I confronted him, and he has never forgiven me for pointing out his sin.

- Paul does not want to share me with friends or family, and this makes me feel isolated.
- Paul does not want to be involved in the deepest things of my heart. For me, this is his most difficult rejection.

Natalie once asked the Lord, "If Paul is not following You, does that nullify my vows?" The response wasn't, "Well, a covenant is a covenant, and he's broken it." It was, "Natalie, what did you mean in your heart?" She knew that she'd vowed before God to join her life to this man, no matter what. A few years later she was ready to leave Paul on what she was sure were biblical grounds. Again she asked God, "Can I leave him now and still be in Your good graces?" She felt God say, "You are always in my good graces. You have grounds, and you may leave. But I wonder, Natalie, if you'd be willing to stay and see what I will do?"

Natalie believed that God asked her to stay and love Paul, so she chose to stay in the marriage. The staying has been painful, but she says, "The hope of seeing what God will do keeps me filled with anticipation." Jeremiah 17:7–8 says:

> Blessed are those who trust in the LORD
> and have made the LORD their hope and confidence.
> They are like trees planted along a riverbank,
> with roots that reach deep into the water.
> Such trees are not bothered by the heat
> or worried by long months of drought.
> Their leaves stay green,
> and they never stop producing fruit. (NLT)

Natalie gives testimony to the truth of this passage. Even in the midst of a very long drought, she and her leaves stay green. I asked her to share with you how this could be and what she would say to a woman in a hard marriage.

The first thing I had to do was forgive Paul. I couldn't do this until I heard a definition of forgiveness that made sense to me.

Forgiveness is releasing someone from your judgment.

First Peter 2:23 began to glow inside of me like an ember. It says, "When they hurled their insults at him, he did not retaliate; when he suffered, he made no threats. Instead, he entrusted himself to him who judges justly" (NIV). Forgiveness means I let go of my own judgment, and I trust God to judge justly.

First I had to forgive, and then I had to walk out love. My Marriage Purpose Statement is a letter I wrote to Paul, stating how I want to live out my love for him. I read it often, asking God to show me how to live it.

My Paul,

I give you my heart, my respect, my acceptance, and my love always regardless of our circumstances or my feelings, for richer, for poorer, in sickness and in health, in agreement and in discord, in peace and in chaos, in joy and in despair.

I will seek to know what is important to you and let that become important to me.

I will tell you the truth to the very best of my ability, and when I find myself hiding, omitting, or distorting the truth, I will return to the simplicity of telling you the truth and trust you and Jesus to handle the ramifications or repercussions. This includes our finances, my emotions, my failures, our children, and my joys.

I will follow our Jesus passionately, fervently, joyfully so that I can be whole in my love for Him and you. I will share with you my discoveries in and with God.

I will let you know me, all of me, every bit that you are willing to know, doing my very best to be transparent for you, that you might find me a trustworthy, safe lover who is without unpleasant secrets.

I will enjoy you just as you are and let any changes that might be necessary in your life be between God and you. I will do my best to allow the Holy Spirit to be your teacher and me to be your cheerleader.

When romance dims, I will do my best to rekindle it, but even if romance burns out, I will continue to love you and be your beloved and friend.

I will keep myself as fit and healthy as I can, that you might find delight in me physically, for I know it is important to you.

I will do my best to make you laugh and never stop singing. I will find joy in you, but do not hold you accountable for my happiness. I will dance and joke and play with you in the good and bad times and will cry and pray and struggle with you in the hard and dark times. I will not leave you or reject you … ever.

And above all, I will ask my Abba for His help and strength always to live and love in the way that is best for us, for you and me as one.

You will be my one and only earthly lover, always.

Your Natalie

I choose to live my Marriage Purpose Statement and to love Paul. Believe me, I don't get to a godly place easily; usually I have a really good gripe first. There are still days I say, "I'm done now, God." But I made a secret choice to stay and watch what God would do. It has been a long, slow walk of loving a man who is not always easy to love. I have peace that I am making a difference, peace that in ten years, twenty years, I will be happy with my choices. BUT today I can see positive change:

- *We are growing as companions.*
- *"Grandma" and "Grandpa" are together and enjoying our first grandchild.*
- *Our marriage is better than it has ever been.*
- *I have hope it will be even better as time goes on.*

What would I say to a woman in a hard marriage? I would encourage her to: Be gentle with yourself. Give yourself grace. Loving someone is not something you achieve. It is something you live, day by day.

Is your marriage in a period of drought where it seems the trial will never end? Plant Jeremiah 17:7–8 in your mind and heart, and make it your prayer to the Lord. I love *The Message*'s paraphrase of these verses:

Blessed is the [woman] who trusts me, God,
*   the woman who sticks with God.*
They're like trees replanted in Eden,
*   putting down roots near the rivers—*
Never a worry through the hottest of summers,
*   never dropping a leaf,*
Serene and calm through droughts,
*   bearing fresh fruit every season.*

Beth Moore writes: "A bruised heart that chooses to beat with passion for God amid pulsing pain and confusion may just be the most expensive offering placed on the divine altar." Natalie has a bruised heart, yet she has slowly seen God pull her and Paul closer together. It hasn't happened in one year; it has been many years, but there is progress and growth toward intimacy. Natalie has chosen to trust God, and she ministers to me and many others with her green leaves. Oh, how God delights in Natalie's expensive offering!

Insight 5: THE INTEGRITY WALK

Tina leaned in close and said, "You would think after so many years of marriage that you'd moved beyond times of crisis. We had many seasons of trials when we were younger, but I thought we'd gotten marriage more together now. Boy, was I wrong."

Jack and Tina had what I call a smooth marriage. They moved easily together without a lot of friction. Then one of their daughters left her husband and moved in with her three children, and a frictionless union became a very uneasy one. As parents, Jack and Tina had agreed on how to raise the children, but they could not agree on their role with the live-in grandchildren. Tension erupted with their daughter. It was no longer a peaceful home.

Beth and Jim had also moved through marriage without too many bumps. Then Jim lost his job. Beth became the "job hunter supervisor," continually checking to make sure Jim was applying for every possible position. Quarrels over money erupted often. The stress of a year with no job threatened to pull Beth and Jim apart.

I can relate to what these couples who have been married many years are going through.

After years of speaking and writing on marriage, I thought I had Jody's and my relationship figured out, and that as we grew older, our intimate oneness would flow easily. But we, too, hit a bump in the road. Children and grandchildren did not move in with us, no one lost a job. After thirty-five years of marriage, we found an area of conflict that we couldn't resolve. It wasn't a moral issue. One of us changed our perspective on something that we had been in agreement about all of our married life. This change disrupted our equanimity and threatened to erode our emotional and spiritual intimacy. Neither Jody nor I ever saw this coming. Marriage wasn't supposed to be like this. It was supposed to get easier. Ha!

God was calling me to trust Him. I promised to choose trust and so I said, *Lord, I choose to trust You for:*

What I don't understand
What doesn't make sense to me
What I can't see.

Was it easy to live with tension at age fifty-five? What do you think?

Did I ever feel like giving up? What do you think?

But I couldn't give up. I wouldn't give up! I had promised to be faithful, to walk in my house with a heart of integrity.

We don't often hear the word *integrity*. It seems like something from George Washington's and John Adams' era. But *integrity* is a word of deep meaning; a biblical word. One dictionary defines *integrity* as "the quality of being honest and upright in character."[6]

The psalmist David said, "I will walk within my house in the integrity of my heart" (Ps. 101:2). This verse speaks of fixed determination. The original Hebrew term translated *integrity* means "to be finished, whole, and complete." It carries with it the idea of being "totally honest, thoroughly sound."[7]

Job offers us the most profound picture of integrity I have ever seen. Almighty God describes Job as "a man of complete integrity" (Job 1:8; 2:3 NLT). He maintained his integrity even when catastrophic trials assailed him (2:3). After all was taken from him—food, property, health, all ten of his children—he still kept his integrity. His wife did not. Job sat with boils covering his body, in physical, emotional, and spiritual agony, and his wife came and asked him, "Are you still trying to maintain your integrity? Curse God and die" (2:9 NLT).

What did Job say to his wife? "You talk like a foolish woman. Should we accept only good things from the hand of God and never anything bad?" (2:10 NLT). Job's idea of maintaining his integrity meant:

Accepting the bad things in life as well as the good.

Do you realize how amazing Job's statement is? In one day he had a tsunami sweep over his possessions and his family, one devastating crash after another. I can't imagine losing one child—and Job lost ten children in one day! He was physically ill, emotionally spent, and questioning spiritually, yet he says, "How can I only accept good? I have been blessed in this life and now the bad has come. I will worship God and bow to Him still" (Job 1:20–21, author's paraphrase).

Job amazes me. I understand why God called him a "man of complete integrity." I want to walk in my house with a heart of integrity. I want to be like Job and worship God, in good times and in hard times.

When I am in pain about something in my marriage, I declare my trust in the Lord out loud to Him. I go to my favorite Scriptures for spiritual help and pray them out loud to God:

> *My Father, I choose to trust You with all my heart, to lean only on You, thanking You that You will straighten out the rough path (see Proverbs 3:5–6).*

> *Lord, I will receive this "irresolvable issue" between Jody and me as a gift. Work endurance and maturity in my life. I want to be like Jesus (see James 1:2–4).*

> *Lord Jesus, thank You that You care affectionately and watchfully for all that concerns me (see 1 Peter 5:7 AB).*

> *Lord, my trust is in You alone. You are my hope and confidence. Oh, please let my leaves stay green … let me continue to bear fruit! (see Jeremiah 17:7–8).*

> *My God, like Job, I will accept the bad along with the good. I will hold fast to my integrity. I trust You! Blessed be Your holy name! (see Job 1:20, 2:10).*

I go to God's Word, and then I take hold of practical helps to fight against trials:

- I put on my Gripes Be Gone bracelet.
- I get out my Thankful Journal and read all the reasons I'm thankful I'm married to this man.
- I practice Philippians 4:8: "I will remember what is true, worthy of respect, honorable, just, pure, lovely. I will dwell on what is excellent and praiseworthy in my husband."
- I get on my knees and read my Marriage Purpose Statement as a prayer to God.

Then I get up off my knees, sigh, and say, *Okay, God, I've got my head on straight now. Show me today how to trust You, and show Jody and me how to grow closer in crisis.*

The story is told of a Green Beret who came up to a speaker after listening to him speak about facing trials together as a couple and said, "In the Green Berets we train over and over, and then over and over again. We repeat some exercises until we are sick of them, but our instructors know what they are doing. They want us so prepared and finely trained that when trials and difficulties come on the battlefield, we will be able to fall back upon that which is second nature to us. We literally learn to do things by reflex action."

Like the Green Berets, let's be prepared for crisis. There are seasons of marriage that seem like a battlefield, but God has given us the battle plan. We are to trust Him, even when we can't see what He is doing. This is what Job did, and his faith in God became worship: "Blessed be the name of the LORD" (Job 1:21).

In the last few years, Jody and I have faced several crises, including my brain injury, his cancer, and this seemingly irresolvable issue. Remember what I said at the beginning of this Dangerous Question about a crisis? We can choose to see a crisis as:

Danger that the crisis will tear us apart and destroy our oneness.

Or we can choose to see …

Opportunity that the crisis will push us together and deepen our oneness.

Jody and I choose that each crisis in our marriage will be an opportunity to grow closer to the Lord and closer to each other. May it be true for you and your husband too!

P.S. Jody and I have now been married forty-six years. Our difference of perspective is still an issue, but we have grown in trusting God. We've gone deeper in accepting and loving each other. That, my friend, is what marriage is all about.

Dangerous Prayer!

My Father, teach me how to trust You. I want crisis to bring my husband and me closer together. I'm up when things are good and down when they're bad. I do want to walk in my house with a heart of integrity.

The Woman in the Mirror

One [woman] has enthusiasm for 30 minutes, another
for 30 days, but it is the [woman] who has it for
30 years who makes a success of [her marriage].
Adapted from Edward B. Butler, *Scientist*

*Every job is a self-portrait of the person who did it.
Autograph your work as a wife with excellence.*
Author Unknown

*The quality of a person's life is in direct
proportion to their commitment to excellence,
regardless of their chosen field of endeavor.*
Vincent T. Lombardi

*Love never fails. Money, youth, and motorboats all fail.
Waistlines stretch, teeth vanish, eyes weaken. Skin wrinkles,
heads bald, arches drop. Love and love alone never gives up.*
William Coleman

Insight 1: LOOK AT YOU … A WIFE BY DESIGN!

National Football League coach John McKay said, "I am a big believer in the *mirror test.* All that matters is if you can look in the mirror and honestly tell the person you see there, that you've done your best." I find the word *best* confusing because some of us feel like we can never live out our definition of "best." If I were writing the above quote, it would sound different—it would go like this:

> *I am a big believer in the mirror test. All that matters is if you can look in the mirror and honestly tell the wife you see there, that you've been faithful.*

Faithfulness is what God asks of me as a wife.

> *It is required that a wife who has been given a trust must prove faithful. (1 Cor. 4:2, author's paraphrase)*

The "trust" I have been given is one man, Jody Dillow, and God asks me to prove trustworthy in carrying out my assignment as a wife to him.

Have you taken this verse into your heart? God doesn't say you have to be the best wife in the world. He doesn't ask you to be successful or popular. You don't have to be like Super Wife down the street. You don't have to be the best lover or best anything. You just have to be the "newly designed you" who says, "Yes, God, I'll ask these Dangerous Questions. Show me what it's like to be married to me." You have taken your assignment as a wife seriously.

Do you know why I respect you? Lots of wives would have put this book back on the shelf and thought, *No way am I asking what it's like to be married to me!* You didn't run from the Dangerous Questions. I think you're brave. I think you're smart. And I just bet you're creative. God is taking brave, smart, creative you and showing you how to love your unique husband. It doesn't happen overnight—it is a process—but you are on the road, headed toward the goal. You, my friend, are becoming a wife by design. You've chosen to live not by default, but by design.

Your design for you as a wife is your Marriage Purpose Statement. You've read the Marriage Statements written by many wives in this book. Every one is special because it is the picture of who each wife longs to become. Your Marriage Statement is unique only to you, designed by God through you to guide you in your journey as a wife. My Marriage Statement has changed over the years, and yours probably will too. Keep it close by, as it is your guide on your journey through the seasons of life as a wife.

I live my years as a wife knowing that one day the Lord will ask me, "Linda, were you faithful?" Faithful wives prove trustworthy in carrying out their assignments. I want to do my part to love Jody, to make the right choices, because one day God will evaluate my life at the judgment seat of Christ. I long to hear the Lord say to me, "Linda, you have loved and encouraged Jody. Well done, My good and faithful servant."

These verses from Psalm 119 have encouraged me as I reflect on walking faithfully as a wife. They encompass all the seasons of my marriage journey: past, present, and future.

> *I have chosen the faithful way....*
> *I cling to Your testimonies....*
> *I shall run the way of Your commandments,*
> *For You will enlarge my heart. (Ps. 119:30–32)*

In the past: **"I have chosen** the faithful way." *Chosen* in Hebrew means to "take a keen look at."[1] It is a choosing that has ultimate and eternal significance. If your choice in the past has been to set your heart on God's desire for your marriage, your choice has eternal significance. God rejoices over your choice! If this has not been your choice in the past, it can be your choice today. Consider writing today's date here:_____.

By doing this, you declare: *From this day forward, I choose God's way. I want to be a wife by design, to live by my Marriage Purpose Statement.*

In the present: **"I cling** to your testimonies." *Cling* is a strong word that means to "stick like glue."[2] This special word is translated as *cleave* in Genesis concerning marriage: "Therefore shall a man leave his father and his mother, and shall cleave unto his wife: and they shall be one flesh" (Gen. 2:24 KJV). I love this; I cling to my husband in intimate oneness, and I cling to God's Word.

In the future: **"I shall run** the way of your commandments." The word *run* fails to capture the energy of the Hebrew word. It means to charge into battle.[3] Your God desires that you have a "charging into battle" mentality as you walk out each day as a wife. With a steadfast heart, determine to keep on keeping on, running purposefully along the track of His commands. Every day you can join me and pray something like this:

> *Okay, God, another day to choose Your way. Give me a charging-into-battle mentality as a wife. Today I will live by my Marriage Purpose Statement.*

Your part is to cling to the faithful way and charge into the battle of becoming all God desires you to be as a wife—to continue running toward who you want to become. This is your part. But the wonderful thing is, God has a part too.

> *I shall run the way of Your commandments,*
> *For You will enlarge my heart.* (Ps. 119:32)

God knows I am weak, and He says to me, "Linda, as you charge into battle, running on My path, I will enlarge your heart by expanding your understanding of Jody. I will multiply your insight into Jody as a man. I will increase your knowledge of how to love and encourage Jody. I will give you skill so you can live your marriage as a thing of beauty." And God's promise is for you, too!

God will enlarge your heart of love for your husband.

God will expand your heart to understand and appreciate him.

God will pump more power into your heart so you can keep on keeping on.

Some people want to give up, but I firmly believe there is no marriage beyond God's healing touch. People give up on marriage, but God doesn't. Sometimes He even takes what we have given up on and re-creates it.

Insight 2: GOD IS THE RE-CREATOR!

Cris and Nick Palafox have personally experienced God's re-creation in their marriage. They *undid* their sacred vows, and then *redid* them again.

> *We were married for nine years.*
> *We were divorced nearly three years.*
> *We remarried April 1998.*
> *We have been given a second chance.*
> *To God be the glory!*[4]

Listen to the sweet messages Nick and Cris wrote to each other. See the joy of God's re-creation!

Nick wrote:

> *Cris, my love, my heart,*
>
> *Thank you for giving me another chance to be your husband, to share our children's lives and our walk with the Lord. Thank you for giving me and the kids so much—no book would have enough room to hold my thanks for who you are and what you mean to me.*

Cris wrote:

Nick, my husband, my love,

Thank you for opening your heart to the Lord and to me. I feel your love, your tender touch, and your forgiveness. You teach, guide, and help me grow. I thank you for accepting His leadership for our family, and for allowing me another chance to be your wife and to make memories with our children as we build our future together.[5]

God is the Re-Creator!

Proverbs 24:3–4 contains a powerful message of hope to wives who want to restore their marriages. It says:

By wisdom a house [of marriage] is built,
And by understanding it is established;
And by knowledge the rooms are filled
With all precious and pleasant riches.

What insight can this passage give you if you want God to restore your marriage? You need to understand three nouns in this verse, but the verbs speak of the possible re-creation of marriage and are even more important.

First, look with me at the nouns: *wisdom, understanding*, and *knowledge.*[6]

"By *wisdom* [a marriage] is built." A wife with wisdom has skill in living life. The Hebrew word used in this passage for wisdom is *hokmah*. In the Old Testament, this word was used to describe the skill of craftsmen, artists, and counselors (Ex. 28:3; 31:3, 6; 35:26; 36:1). Wisdom is skill, a skill in living life as a thing of beauty. A wife who lives skillfully helps create a marriage of lasting value.

"By *understanding* [a marriage] is established." A wife with understanding listens to her husband's heart. She weighs her words on the balance scale of love.

"By *knowledge* the rooms are filled with all precious and pleasant riches." A wife with knowledge studies her husband and asks, "Who is he today, my Lord? Who is he becoming? Show me what encouragement looks like during this season of his life."

Now for the exciting part—the three verbs: *built, established,* and *filled.*

"By wisdom [a marriage] is *built.*" The Hebrew word translated here as *built* suggests the idea of restoring. It is the idea of "*re*"building something so that it flourishes once again.[7] When you said, "I'll look in the mirror and ask, *What's it like to be married to me?*" you took a step to begin the rebuilding process.

"By understanding [a marriage] is *established.*" The word *established* means to "set in order."[8] It's the idea of putting something back into an upright position, something that was once leaning, falling, or twisted. This is exactly what you have been doing. You've taken each Dangerous Question and said:

> *Change me, God. Take me from griping to gratitude.*
> *Change me, God. I long to give my body as a gift to my husband.*
> *Change me, God. I want to forgive freely as Christ forgave me.*

"By knowledge the rooms are *filled* with all precious and pleasant riches." The word *filled* suggests fulfillment and abundant satisfaction. These riches are not of this world but are found in the precious and pleasant joy of a deep intimacy between you and your husband. I pray this is growing in your marriage.

My friend, do you understand this message of hope? It isn't about already-perfect relationships. This is about restoring and rebuilding a relationship so it can once again flourish. It is about taking a marriage that has been leaning, almost falling over, and re-creating it so it can stand strong. So it is lasting.

Oh, I hope you see. This passage is saying that there is always hope. If you feel discouraged about your marriage, STOP! There is hope! If you feel like it is impossible to be the wife God asks you to be, STOP! There is hope! *God is in the re-creation business. That means there is hope for you and for your marriage.*

God says hope comes through His Word and through the Holy Spirit (Rom. 15:4, 13). Read God's promises from His Word again on the previous pages. They are for you! Wherever your marriage is today, there is hope because God breathes hope through the Word and the Spirit. He is the God of hope!

Insight 3: THE CHANGING SEASONS OF YOUR MARRIAGE

Every couple travels on a journey though the changing seasons of their marriage. Some seasons we skip through as they are joyous and filled with delight. Others we stomp through, hoping they are quickly over. And some we walk through on tippy toes because we long to embrace every moment of the tender intimate oneness.

Jody and I began our marriage journey as young, idealistic college students. We were new Christians and convinced that with Christ as Lord of our marriage, it would be a walk in the park. So, we wrapped our arms around one another and began walking through the seasons of our lover/best-friend intimacy together. Quickly, we learned that all seasons were not a stroll in the park. So, we whispered words of encouragement to one another. Sometimes, when our partner struggled, we shouted words to build them up: "I love you; I'm here for you; we'll get through this together."

I began writing to you about Dangerous Questions on Jody's and my forty-fifth anniversary. Amazingly enough, another year has passed. God gives us anniversaries as milestones, significant points in the passing of time, specific yet mute reminders that more sand has passed through the hourglass. He builds them into our calendar once every year to enable us to make an annual appraisal—not of the length of time we've been married but the depth of our intimacy. Not just to remind us we've been married longer, but to help us determine if we are now married deeper.

Jody and I have grown deeper in our intimate oneness, and I thank and praise God. I wrote a letter to God on our last anniversary to express my gratitude for His molding of two very different people into one. Even though the letter was to God, I gave it to Jody in his anniversary card.

My Father,

It is our forty-sixth anniversary, and my heart is filled with thankfulness to You. I woke up this morning wanting to write You, precious Lord, to thank You for Your abundant wisdom. I am so grateful for this husband You brought to me. You knew, You saw, that even though we were so different, that we would learn to complement and complete one another.

I laugh when I think how the first year of our marriage I said to Jody, "You should have a wife more like you; an intellect, someone interested in deep theology." And I really believed that. And Jody was convinced I needed a husband who was more social, more structured, more of everything he wasn't.

How beautiful it is to look back over the seasons of our marriage and see the beauty of Your choice for me. Would marriage have been a smoother ride through the decades with someone else? Maybe. But together Jody and I have learned to live the words adapt, accept, respect, and love—as Christ loved, with no strings attached. We have grown more intimate with You, our God, as we have begged You for answers, listened to Your gentle whispers as

You painted a picture of just what love looked like for our mate that very day.

Oh, look at the lover/best-friend intimacy we have forged! It takes my breath away!

On this day when I pledged to love, honor, and respect Jody Dillow, I bow and thank You, my God. I am so blessed!

Your Linda

I think it is helpful for each of us to see how other couples walk on their marriage journey, to reflect on how other wives live by intentional design. So, I want to introduce you to three couples at different places in their journey together: one in the morning of their marriage, one in the late afternoon, and the last in the midnight hours of their marriage. Each couple has committed to be forever faithful, although what that means looks different for each of them. Each has experienced seasons of difficulty and grown more in love through the hard times.

Heidi and Scott White are a picture of young love. They have been married six years. Below is Heidi's Marriage Purpose Statement, which is based on a passage from the Song of Solomon:

> *Place me like a seal over your heart,*
> *Like a seal on your arm;*
> *For love is as strong as death,*
> *Its jealousies unyielding as the grave.*
> *It burns like blazing fire,*
> *Like a mighty flame.*
> *Many waters cannot quench love;*
> *Rivers cannot wash it away.*
> *If one were to give all the wealth of his house for love,*
> *It would be utterly scorned. (Song 8:6–7)*

My marriage goal is that I would choose every day of my life to intentionally see Scott through the lens of the love described in Song of Solomon 8:6–7.

- *I will prioritize Scott as first in all my human relationships.*
- *I will listen to Scott.*
- *I will study Scott.*
- *I will honor Scott in word and action.*

Heidi and Scott are basking in the morning sunshine of their marriage, yet they think on deep things. We see in the passage Heidi used for her Marriage Purpose Statement that nothing can quench this love. Why? "Its flashes are flashes of fire, the very flame of the LORD" (Song 8:6).

May the flame of the Lord light a fire in your heart for your husband.

The second couple, Bev and Gary DeSalvo, are in the afternoon of their marriage. They have been married thirty-two years. Here is Bev's Marriage Purpose Statement:

When I look into the mirror I see an image of myself. It is an exact likeness of Bev DeSalvo, and it's the only way I know if my makeup is smooth and if the cowlick in the back of my hair is filled in. In fact, it is the only way that I can know what I look like from the chest up.

Ephesians 5:31–32 tells us that our marriage is to be a mysterious reflection of Christ and the Church. So when people look at my marriage, I want them to see a divine representation of the love relationship between the Beloved Bridegroom and His bride, whose hearts are knit together so tightly that God sees them as one. My desire is to become so close to my husband that we are spiritually, emotionally, and physically one. So I choose to trust Gary DeSalvo and allow him to lead me in a holy, romantic dance for all the days that we have left on earth together. I surrender to the

Holy One so that I can hear Him tell me how to listen to Gary's heart when he speaks, and not just his words. I will keep my eyes on my Beloved so that I will know when, where, and how to step in time with Gary as our bodies, hearts, and minds become so closely woven together that Abba sees us as one flesh. I pray that as He mysteriously knits us together we will reflect an image of the passionate love relationship between Christ and His bride. Who knows? This may be the only way someone will know what that looks like.

I love Bev's word picture of God mysteriously knitting husband and wife together so their union will radiate the joyous and passionate intimacy between Christ and His bride. It's as if God elevates the marriage bond by declaring, "Look at Bev and Gary—look at Jody and Linda—and catch a glimpse of Me—Jesus—with my bride, the Church." I am humbled. Can the world see holy love in the way I love Jody—in the tone of my voice when I speak to him, in the joy of my smile when I look at him?

May the world see the mysterious reflection of Christ and the Church in your intimate oneness and mine.

Young love is vital and energizing, love in the afternoon years is stable and secure, but the question is asked:

Is there anything more beautiful in life than a boy and a girl clasping clean hands and pure hearts in the path of marriage? Can there be anything more beautiful than young love? And the answer is given. "Yes, there is a more beautiful thing. It is the spectacle of an old man and an old woman finishing their journey together on that path. Their hands are gnarled, but still clasped; their faces are seamed but still radiant; their hearts are physically bowed and tired, but still strong with love and devotion for one another. Yes, there is a more beautiful thing than young love: old love."[9]

The third couple, Mark and Anita Bubeck, are in the midnight of their marriage. They show us a portrait of the beauty of old love. Mark is a Christian leader and author, yet God has given him a new job, caring for his wife of sixty years. For the last ten years, Alzheimer's has slowly been taking Anita away. Mark is still able to care for her in their home.

The Bubecks' daughter, my friend Judy Dunagan, wrote this touching poem after visiting her parents:

The Dance

Their dance took my breath away.
Heads bowed toward each other, face to face.
She in a pink bathrobe, her hands gripped on her walker.
He is gently coaxing her to take steps toward him as he guides the
*   front of her walker.*
He is guiding her toward her hospital bed,
Placed recently at the foot of the bed they've shared for almost 60
*   years of marriage.*
She is breathing heavily as if she's run a marathon,
Taking only ten steps from the bathroom where her
Husband just helped her like she helped me when I was a
*   toddler.*
He gently helps her into her new bed.
She looks at him with frightened, childlike eyes and says,
"I am afraid." He says, "Don't be afraid, Jesus is here."
He tucks her in while they quietly sing "His Name is
*   Wonderful!"*
She still remembers most of the words of this favorite hymn.
Her voice is still beautiful and she sings on key.
He brushes her cheek with a gentle kiss,

And covers her with his prayers.
He then goes to their bed alone.
With his bride in her hospital bed at the foot of his bed,
She soon falls asleep, safely under the shelter of him.[10]

I can't read "The Dance" without tears. What a precious picture of lifetime love. Judy says that the first night of her visit she couldn't take her eyes off of them as her dad so lovingly cared for his bride. While cleaning their home, Judy found a note her mom probably wrote two years ago, before Alzheimer's stole her beautiful handwriting. On a yellow sticky note she had written, "I'm fading away, but Jesus is keeping me every day."

May we experience the precious joy of "Old Love."

In the beginning of your marriage journey you pledged:

For better or worse, for richer or poorer, in sickness and in health.

When we are young, beautiful, and vital, our ears are attuned to BETTER, RICHER, and HEALTH. But each couple will enter into seasons of WORSE, POORER, and SICKNESS.

Jody and I have known sickness. He sat by my bed for five days in the trauma hospital in California after my fall and brain injury. I was "not there," so he sat and held my hand and prayed. I've had my turn to pray as I followed the ambulance in the middle of the night to the emergency room when Jody's heart wasn't working right, when his pacemaker failed. In a week, I will hold his hand and pray after his cancer surgery.

When you are young and strong, it doesn't sound difficult to say, "In sickness and in health." Health is definitely more fun than sickness, for better is lots more fun than for worse, and we all know richer is more fun than poorer. But I committed to the bad as well as to the good. Jody and I have known both.

Marriage is a journey. I want to walk through the seasons of my marriage with a forever-faithful mentality. So I brand the words of 1 Corinthians 13 on my heart and make a secret choice to live them:

> *Love never gives up, never loses faith, is always hopeful, and endures through every circumstance. (1 Cor. 13:7 NLT)*

There is glorious hope for those who choose to faithfully endure through every season of marriage. I believe this will be your choice!

Insight 4: LOOK AT YOU: LEARNING! GROWING! CHANGING!

Ten women, married seven to fifteen years, sat around the table holding their Marriage Purpose Statements. As they each read the portrait of who they wanted to become as a wife, I was unprepared for their waves of emotion. As Renee began reading hers, tears fell, and she stopped. She gathered herself together and read, only to stop a second time. Renee's good friend tried to come to the rescue—"I'll read it for Renee." I smiled at sweet Renee and said, "I think Renee can read it."

Here is what she read:

> *I pray that one day soon I can be this person for my God and for my husband.*

As Read by David

> *You raised me up, so I could stand on mountains,*
> *You made me want to be a better man.*
> *My head turned only in your direction and*
> *your laughter made me stare with delight.*
> *Your confidence made my breath escape*
> *And your passion for GOD and me was so great.*

Your heart always growing
the capacity never full
the kindness you showed was unconditional.
You were perfect from your head all the way to your toes.
You raised me up more than you'll ever know.
The Lord was her love and I was her lover.

As Renee finished reading, she looked up at the group and said through her tears, "I read this to David last night. My poem to him was about how I wanted him to see me by the end of my life, but when I read it, David was so sweet. He was really touched by the poem and looked at me as if to say, 'I already think of you that way,' where I feel like I still have a long way to go."

Two days later, her husband flew to Haiti with Compassion International to film children in Haiti's villages. When the earthquake of 2010 hit Haiti, David had just walked into Hotel Montana. An unending month later, David's body was found among the rubble. He was one of more than two hundred thousand who perished.

During David's memorial service, the pastor called Renee up to the stage. He told the five hundred gathered to celebrate David's life that Renee had written her Marriage Purpose Statement and read it to David before he left for Haiti. As the pastor read Renee's poem, there wasn't a dry eye in the sanctuary. Here was a wife who lived intentionally in her marriage—who thought about what was really important to her and who verbalized who she wanted to become to God and to her husband.

After her husband's death Renee said, "I'm so grateful that one of the last things David heard from me was my Marriage Purpose Statement. He knew who I wanted to be to him as a wife and that I was walking toward that goal."

David Hames was forty years old when he died. We don't expect life to end when we're young, when our sons are ages three and six. We all feel like we have all the time in the world, but God's Word tells us differently.

Lord, remind me how brief my time on earth will be.
 Remind me that my days are numbered—
 how fleeting my life is.
You have made my life no longer than the width of my hand.
 My entire lifetime is just a moment to you;
 at best, each of us is but a breath. (Ps. 39:4–5 NLT)

This life is short, and so we want to grow every day toward who we want to become. The minutes of our marriage pass so quietly, so consistently, that we fail to realize the time is ticking away, so I go back to where I started: We must live our marriage by design. We only have this year, this month, this moment to grow in intimate oneness.

Can you remember back to the first chapter where you thought about what was really important to you? I asked you to think about your funeral, thirty years in the future, and imagine what you would want your husband to say about you as a wife. Then you wrote your Marriage Purpose Statement. Why don't you get your Marriage Statement and read it now. I wonder, as you think back to all the Dangerous Questions you have asked yourself as you have read this book—is there anything you would change in what you wrote? Ask the Lord if there is anything He wants you to change.

Think deeply, because "one of these days, much sooner than you want to face, one of you is going to be sitting beside the deathbed of the other, holding a frail, clammy hand. You'll look into each other's misty eyes during those aching, final hours, and the memories will flood through your grieving minds in a raging torrent.

- You will not regret a single dreamy walk you took together in the park.
- You will not regret the time you stayed up so late talking and holding each other that you were both zombies at work the next day.

- You will not regret all the times you made love and let the housework go."[11]

And more than that—

- You will not regret writing your Marriage Purpose Statement and sharing it with your husband.
- You will not regret telling your husband why you respect him.

But I'll tell you what you will regret.

- You will regret the hundreds of hours you spent fighting.
- You will regret the times you held a grudge or gave the silent treatment.
- You will regret griping, venting, and complaining.
- You will regret saying, "Maybe next year sex will get better."
- You will regret not really believing that your time as lovers was limited.

I don't think you will regret looking in the mirror. I am a big believer in the *mirror test*. All that matters is if you can look in the mirror and honestly say to yourself these three words: *I've been faithful.*

Look in the mirror! I think you will see a "newly designed wife," a brave woman who is intentionally becoming her picture of a faithful wife. Keep on learning. Keep on growing. Keep on changing. Your intimacy with that special man, your husband, will just get better and more beautiful!

Know that I will be praying for you as you keep on keeping on.

A Ten- (or Twelve-) Week Reflective Bible Study

To the Women in This Study:

I'm excited that you are willing to ask, *What's it like to be married to me?* and to reflect on the other Dangerous Questions. You are taking a step forward in becoming a wife by design. This is exciting!

I've called this a reflective Bible study, because it is a bit different from a normal Bible study. It is:

- A time to think deeply about who you are as a wife—and who you are becoming.
- A time to be in God's Word, reading, pondering, and memorizing.
- A time to think, search your soul, pray, and plan.
- A time to do practical projects that will reveal to you much about you, your husband, and your marriage.

Before you begin, here are some things you need to know:

1. Each Bible study has the questions divided under five days. Some of these line up with the Dangerous Questions' insights; others do not. You can do the study all at once or over five days or three days or seven days, whatever works for you.

2. Some sections have personal projects for you to do. If so, I alert you at the beginning of the study so you can have the entire week to work on the project.

3. What you put into the Bible study and the projects is what you will get out—growth takes work, reflection takes quiet, time, and thought.

Thank you for setting these weeks aside to reflect on your marriage and who you are becoming as a wife. I am asking the Lord to meet with you, to send His Blessed Spirit as Teacher, Encourager, Comforter, and Transformer!

I am praying for you!

Linda Dillow, 2010

To the Bible Study Leader:

I'm excited you are going to lead the reflective Bible study on *What's It Like to Be Married to Me?* Let me give you a little of my thinking about a few things in the study.

I stress memorizing God's Word because our minds are renewed when they are filled with God's truth.

I ask the women in the study to write out Scripture because when we write, we see things we missed by simply reading. For the same reason, I often ask the women to read the Word out loud.

In the first three studies I assign some projects. Be sure to alert the women in your study to the project so they will have the entire week to reflect, practice, and complete the project. In the second Bible study, the women are to wear a "Gripes Be Gone" bracelet all week. Every time they gripe, they have to change the bracelet to the other arm. Each day they journal about what they learn about themselves and about *when* they complain. The bracelet is available at www.LindaDillow.org. The bracelet will bring life changes but also add an element of fun.

I encourage wives to have a Thankful Journal where they can record what they are learning about growing in God gratitude and in husband gratitude. You can either buy some journals and have the women pay you, or let them get their own. In the future, I hope to have Thankful Journals available on the website. On the website, you will find additional examples of Marriage Purpose Statements plus comments from women who have taken the Bible study. Please email the website with anything you or your group feel would be helpful for other Bible study groups.

The study can be either ten or twelve weeks. Ten of the lessons correspond to the Dangerous Questions in the book. The two additional studies are a time of thanksgiving, reflection, and celebration. These optional studies fall after weeks five and ten. My hope in having the study be ten or twelve weeks was to make it adaptable for every group, but if possible, I encourage you to do the two additional studies, as I believe they push God's truth deeper into hearts.

When I led the pilot studies for this book, I told the study groups that they could share anything about themselves as a wife, but they could *not* share anything about their husbands—unless, of course, it was positive. This study is for wives. It's an invitation for them to ask themselves Dangerous Questions, to seek God and His perspective. It is a place to begin to live, not by default, but by design. To look ahead and decide who you want to become, and then begin to grow toward that picture.

Know that I am praying for you as you lead your precious women to all God desires them to be as wives.

I trust the Lord to lead you as you lead them!

Linda Dillow, 2010

Week 1

What Is Really Important to Me?

Read "By Design, Not Default" and "What Is Really Important to Me?". Focus on Insight 5 in "What Is Really Important to Me?" (pages 30–34) so you can be reflecting on it all week.

"By Design, Not Default," Day 1: By Design or Default?
1. What did you learn (both positive and negative) in your childhood home about marriage?

2. Describe a woman who was a role model to you as a wife.

3. Why did you choose this woman as your picture of a wife?

Memorize and meditate on Song of Solomon 5:16

> "*His mouth is full of sweetness*
> *And he is wholly desirable.*
> *This is my beloved and this is my friend.*"

4. Write a paragraph amplifying what this verse says to you personally.

"What Is Really Important to Me?", Day 1: What Do My Choices Say?

1. What do you say is most important to you? List your priorities.

2. How would your husband list your priorities?

3. How would it help you to ask yourself, *Will I be happy with my choice in five years or twenty years?*

Day 2: Marriage Matters and The Treadmill Won't Stop

> *It is because the LORD is acting as the witness between you and the wife of your youth, because you have broken faith with her, though she is your partner, the wife of your marriage covenant.*

Has not the LORD made them one? In flesh and spirit they are his…. So guard yourself in your spirit, and do not break faith with the wife of your youth. (Mal. 2:14–15 NIV)

1. How would you explain these verses to a young woman about to marry?

2. How can you "guard yourself in your spirit"?

3. Reflect on Bethany and Chris's marriage vows on pages 23–24. When you read these precious vows, do you feel joyful, sad, encouraged, or discouraged? What do your feelings say to you?

4. Which of the comments on pages 26–27 do you identify with? Why?

5. What can you do to get off the treadmill?

Day 3: Live with the End in View

1. Do you agree with Emily's statement in the play *Our Town* that no one ever realizes life while they live it? Explain your answer.

2. Are you living in reality, valuing each day with your husband, or are you walking through marriage as in a fog?

3. Read Psalm 90:12 and Ephesians 5:15–16. Write a paragraph describing how living these verses will help you realize life while you live it.

4. Find a block of time and a quiet place. Reflect on what you would want your husband to say at your funeral thirty years from now. (Refer to the questions on page 30.) Write your thoughts in a notebook or journal.

Day 4: Aim for the Goal

1. Define a goal

2. Define a desire

3. Have you had your goals and desires mixed up? If so, how?

Day 5: Get a Vision for Your Marriage

Now it is your turn to write your unique Marriage Purpose Statement.

Find a quiet place and time to reflect. Review what you wrote about what you want your husband to say at your funeral thirty years from now. These words describe who you hope to become. Think, pray, and form your thoughts into a Marriage Purpose Statement. It can be a:

- Resolution or declaration
- Prayer
- Scripture
- Poem or song
- Letter you write to yourself
- Acrostic
- List or paragraph

Come prepared to share your personal Marriage Purpose Statement at the Bible study.

Week 2

What Does It Feel Like to Be My Husband?

Read "What Does It Feel Like to Be My Husband?", Insight 5 now. Begin wearing your bracelet and journaling today.

Day 1: Sophisticated Venting

Memorize Philippians 2:14 in any translation of the Bible (and 15 and 16 if you can!).

> *Do everything without complaining and arguing, so that no one can criticize you. (v. 14–15 NLT)*

> *Live clean, innocent lives as children of God, shining like bright lights in a world full of crooked and perverse people. (v. 15 NLT)*

1. What are your thoughts as you read what wives said was the worst thing they had done in their marriage (see pages 44–45)?

2. Do you think you are a positive person, a griping nag, or somewhere in between? Explain your answer.

3. If you haven't already, begin wearing your bracelet and journaling today. What do you learn about yourself as you wear and switch the bracelet? Be specific.

Day 2: Where Did I Catch the Griping Disease?

1. Read page 47 and then write your own translation of Philippians 4:8.

2. List at least five things you learn from Jean's story on pages 48–49.

3. Do you think Christian women think it is okay to whine and complain? Give an example.

Day 3: God—on Griping

1. Read Proverbs 27:15–16 and write the verses here.

2. Read Proverbs 25:24 and write it here.

3. Give an example of when you have been "the nag."

4. Read Proverbs 12:4 and write it here.

5. Read Proverbs 31:11–12 and write it here.

6. Give an example of when you have been "the crown."

Day 4: Gripes Be Gone!

1. Read 1 Corinthians 10:1–13. Write your own paraphrase of this passage.

2. Who were the Israelites really griping about? How do you do this?

Day 5: Put on a Bracelet

1. Read Psalm 142:1–5. List your complaints before the Lord. Write them here.

2. Read Romans 15:5–7. Apply these verses by writing a prayer about accepting your husband.

3. Read Matthew 7:3–5. Pray and ask God to show you how to fill in the following chart.

His Faults	My Wrong Responses

4. Write a prayer, giving God permission to change you (instead of asking Him to change your husband).

Using a "Gripes Be Gone" bracelet, take the challenge for a week. Every time a gripe or complaint escapes your lips, switch the bracelet to your other wrist. Be sure to journal every day about what you are learning about yourself through this project.

Day 1

Day 2

Day 3

Day 4

Day 5

Day 6

Day 7

Week 3

Am I Willing to Change My Attitude?

Buy a special journal to be your Thankful Journal, or use any journal or notebook.

Day 1: Building a House of Gratitude
1. Memorize Psalm 92:1–2. Write Psalm 92:1–2 here.

2. Read about Kaye on page 65. If you were going to list three things you would do to nurture an attitude of gratitude, what would they be?

Day 2: Growing in God Gratitude
Make Psalm 92:1–2 your daily practice this week. Thank and praise God in the morning for His lovingkindness and in the evening for His faithfulness. Journal what you are learning each day in your Thankful Journal.

Day 3: Growing in Husband Gratitude
Read about the Thankful Journal on pages 75–76. Chose one day this week

to write in your journal about why you are thankful for your husband. (Consider sharing what you write with your husband.)

Read "Dwell on the positive" on page 76. Then list the following words from Philippians 4:8 in your Thankful Journal: *true, worthy of respect, right, pure, lovely, excellent, worthy of praise*. Each day of the week, dwell on one of these attributes and ask God the Spirit to reveal how your husband displays this quality. Write your thoughts in your Thankful Journal.

1. Gratitude creates an atmosphere where emotional sweetness can flourish. Write a paragraph describing what it looks like in your marriage when sweetness reigns.

Day 4: Offer a Sacrifice of Thanksgiving

1. Read Emma's story of offering a sacrifice of thanksgiving on pages pages 81–83. Write a paragraph that describes the feelings and thoughts you have as you read this.

2. Read Psalm 50:14–15, 23 and Hebrews 13:15. Write a summary of the four verses and how they apply personally to you and your marriage.

Day 5: A Dangerous Prayer!

The book of Colossians has four chapters, and each one talks about being thankful. Read each of these references: Colossians 1:3, 12; 2:7; 3:15–17; 4:2. In your Thankful Journal, personalize the thankful message to your husband.

1. What does it look like for you to devote yourself to prayer for your husband with an alert mind and a thankful heart? Write your answer here.

Week 4

What Will It Take for Me to Get Close to You? Part 1

Day 1: Surprise! Men and Women Are Different!

1. Memorize Genesis 2:18. Write it here.

2. Write your description of emotional intimacy.

3. Consider asking your husband how he would define emotional intimacy. Write his answer here.

4. List three ways you can move closer to your "shoulder to shoulder" husband.

Day 2: We Both Have Gaps

Prayerfully read Ephesians 5:25–32.

1. Do you see any conditions the wife must meet before her husband loves her sacrificially?

2. Do you see any conditions the husband must meet before the wife respects him unconditionally?

3. Fill in the commands you find in Ephesians 5:25–32 in the chart below.

Commands to Husband	Commands to Wife

4. Whose commands are the most difficult to live out, the husband's or the wife's? Why?

Day 3: A Wife's Divine Calling

1. How do you describe your "love gap"? Use at least three words.

2. How do you describe your husband's "respect gap"? Use at least three words.

3. Memorize Ephesians 5:33 in *The Amplified Bible:*

> *And let the wife see that she respects and reverences her husband [that she notices him, regards him, honors him, prefers him, venerates, and esteems him; and that she defers to him, praises him, and loves and admires him exceedingly].*

4. It is very difficult for some wives to live out this description of the word respect. Give five reasons why you think it is hard.

Day 4: A Wife's Divine Calling

1. What did you learn in your childhood family about being a "helper"?

2. Write out the following verses about God being our Ezer, our strong Helper: Psalm 121:1–2; 124:8; 146:5. Then read them out loud as a prayer of thanksgiving to God.

3. Write a paragraph describing what it looks like practically for you to respect your unique husband unconditionally.

Day 5: A Wife's Divine Calling

1. Does learning about the word Ezer (page 97) help you with being called a "helper"? Give five reasons why.

2. What do you learn from Tamra about being a helper (page 98)?

3. Write a letter to your daughter, niece, granddaughter, or other special young woman in your life. Share with her about a wife's divine calling to be an Ezer—a helper to her husband.

Week 5

What Will It Take for Me to Get Close to You? Part 2

Day 1: Fill His Gaps with Encouragement and Respect

1. Memorize Ephesians 4:29. Write it here.

2. In Ephesians 4:29, there is one negative command and three positive commands. List them.

3. Tell about a time when you encouraged your husband with your words.

4. Read 1 Thessalonians 5:11 out loud. Ask God to show you at least five ways you can build up and encourage your special husband with your actions. List them.

TAKE THE RESPECT TEST!

- Find a quiet place.
- Spend ten or fifteen minutes making a list of things you respect about your husband.
- When your husband is not distracted, say, "I was thinking about you today and several things about you that I respect, and I just want you to know that I respect you."
- Leave the room, and leave the response up to God.
- How did your husband respond? Describe how your words and actions impacted your husband.

Look at the acrostic of the word respect on page 105, then make your own acrostic of respect. Perhaps you would like to frame it or keep a copy in your Bible where you can reflect on it often. Consider sharing your acrostic with your husband and telling him you want to learn to live it.

Day 2: Who Will Fill My Gaps?

1. What do you think are your husband's five most basic needs?

2. What are your five greatest needs?

3. Do you think you and your husband understand each other's needs?

Consider sharing the lists you wrote with him and asking for his input.

4. Read Matthew 20:28. How does this verse relate to you as a wife?

5. Read about changing your perspective from my right to God's gift on page 106. Write a paragraph explaining this concept to a friend.

Day 3: Who Will Fill My Gaps?

1. Read Michelle's story at least two times (pages 107–109). If you were making a list of things you were giving to God, what would be on your list?

2. Write an email to a friend expressing what you learned from Michelle's story. Explain what difference you think this will make in your marriage.

3. Read Philippians 2:3–4. If possible, read these verses in other translations. Write the verses here.

4. Meditate on Philippians 2:3–4. Then write your own paraphrase of these verses, applying them to your role as a wife.

Day 4: Who Will Fill My Gaps?

1. Read "What Will It Take for Me to Get Close to You?", Insight 6, "A Wife Can Set the Stage for Intimacy" (pages 109–114). Ask the Lord to speak to you personally from this insight.

2. Read the description of emotional sweetness on page 109. What do you think your husband would say is the opposite of emotional sweetness? Consider asking him.

Day 5: A Wife Can Set the Stage for Intimacy

Read again "A Wife Can Set the Stage for Intimacy" (page 109–114). You are a wife, and that means that just like Krista, *you* can set the stage for intimacy.

Pray, and ask the Lord to speak to you and reveal what will speak love to your husband.

Ask God to show you if a weekend away, a day hike, a once-in-a-lifetime vacation, just you two, or a day of cross-country skiing will build emotional intimacy between you and your husband.

1. Krista ministered to Caleb body, soul, and spirit. Write down how she did this, and ask God to show you if any of these ideas are right for your husband.

You, dear wife, with God's guidance set the stage for intimacy. Step out and do it!

Optional Lesson for a Twelve-Week Study

A Time of Thanksgiving, Reflection, and Celebration

You have been asking yourself Dangerous Questions for the last five weeks. You have searched God's Word and reflected on who you want to become. You are on the road to becoming a wife by design, not default, and that is exciting! This week will be a time of thanksgiving, reflection, and celebration.

THANKSGIVING (TO BE DONE ON YOUR OWN, PRIOR TO THE MEETING)
Reflect on Psalm 92:1–2, the verses you memorized the week you reflected on the Dangerous Question *Am I willing to change my attitude?* In the morning, you thanked and praised God for His lovingkindness and in the evening for His faithfulness. Make this your habit again this week.

REFLECTION (FOR YOUR STUDY DURING THE FIVE DAYS OF THE WEEK)
Day 1: Look through the first Dangerous Question, *What is* really *important to me?* Read through the first Bible study, thanking and praising God that you are living not by default, but by design. Ask God to show you one way you've grown because you asked, *What is really important to me?*

Day 2: Reflect on the second Dangerous Question, *What does it feel like to be my husband?* Page through the chapter and read over the Bible study. Put on your "Gripes Be Gone" bracelet and thank God that your venting and complaining is different than it was five weeks ago. Ask God to show you one way you've grown because you asked, *What does it feel like to be my husband?*

Day 3: The third Dangerous Question was about attitude: *Am I willing to change my attitude?* Think about how you've grown in God gratitude and husband gratitude. Look through the entries in your Thankful

Journal and thank God that gratitude is growing in you. Ask God to show you one way you've changed because you asked, *Am I willing to change my attitude?*

Day 4: Reflect on the fourth Dangerous Question, *What will it take for me to get close to you?* Scan-read the chapter again and read through the Bible study. Remember that God has a special calling on your life—to be an *Ezer*, a helper to your husband. Encouragement and respect are beginning to flow from you to him. You are learning to fill his respect gap. Ask God to show you one way you are different because you asked, *What will it take for me to get close to you?*

Day 5: Continue to reflect on how to set the stage for intimacy. Reread how Krista set the stage and filled her husband to overflowing, body, soul, and spirit (page 110). Ask God to show you how you can set the stage for intimacy with your husband.

CELEBRATION (to be done prior to and during your group time)
As you look back and thank God and reflect on what He has been teaching you, think of something to prepare to share with the group during your celebration time.

Your time of celebration will be during your next Bible study. Decide in advance as a group how this time will look. You could have a brunch or luncheon or meet outside if the weather is nice. Allow time for each woman to share how this study has impacted her view of God and of her marriage. Here are six suggestions for what you could do to prepare:

1. Read something you wrote for an assignment.

2. Write a letter to your daughter (daughter-in-law, grand-daughter, niece, special friend), expressing what you have learned as you've reflected on the first five Dangerous Questions.

3. Make an acrostic using a word like marriage, intimacy, or wife.

4. Recite memory verses that have been meaningful to you.

5. Draw a graph that shows how you have grown.

6. Write a poem or a song or paint a picture that reveals what God has taught you.

End with a time of worship and prayer, celebrating what God has done. And you still have four more Dangerous Questions ahead!

Week 6

What Is It Like to Make Love with Me? Part 1

This week you will ponder and reflect on:

1. How your sexual mind-set developed, and what it is today.

2. What the Song of Solomon teaches about God's perspective of sexual intimacy.

Day 1: How Did We Get Where We Are?

1. What did you learn in your home about sexual intimacy in marriage?

2. How did this influence you when you married?

3. "A mind-set is a collection of individual thoughts that over a period of time influence the way we perceive life."[1] How have your individual thoughts over the past twenty years (or more) contributed to the sexual mind-set you have today?

4. Which of Satan's lies about your sexuality did you listen to (page 118)?

5. How were you influenced by the media (page 118)?

6. Did Christians influence you in a positive or negative way (page 119)?

7. After reading this chapter, how do you think your sexual mind-set differs from God's perspective?

Day 2: Open the Gift of Sexual Passion

God gave the gift of sexual passion for an intimate oneness.

1. Read and memorize Ephesians 5:31–32. Write it here.

2. Paraphrase these verses here.

3. Ephesians 5:31–32 says that your sexual intimacy is a picture of the spiritual intimacy the Lord desires with you. How does this change how you view intimacy with your husband?

God gave the gift of sexual passion for exquisite pleasure.

4. Read Proverbs 5:15, 18–19. Paraphrase Proverbs 5:19 here.

Day 3: Open the Gift of Sexual Passion

1. Read Proverbs 5:15, 18–19 again. List five to ten adjectives that describe this wife as a sexual partner.

2. Read Song of Solomon 7:1–9. Write a paragraph describing what you see in this bride as a lover.

3. Make a list of what Claire did to open the gift of sexual passion.

4. If you put as much thought, prayer, and creativity into your sexual intimacy as Claire did, where would you be as a lover to your husband?

Days 4 & 5: Open the Gift of Sexual Passion

Read the Song of Solomon. If possible, read it in a modern version like the New Living Translation.

The theme of the Song is found in Song of Solomon 8:6:

> *Put me like a seal over your heart,*
> *Like a seal on your arm.*
> *For love is as strong as death,*
> *Jealousy is as severe as Sheol;*
> *Its flashes are flashes of fire,*
> *The very flame of the LORD.*

"This, the key verse of the Song, speaks of a love between a husband and wife that is white-hot, passionate, burning, and unable to be extinguished because it comes from God."[2]

Here are three reasons given for why the Song of Solomon can be confusing:[3]

> 1. We don't understand how to read Hebrew poetry. It helps
> to realize that you are reading poetry and not prose. The
> beauty of God writing this love poem through Solomon
> exactly the way He did in poetic symbols is so precious; a
> child can pick up the Song of Solomon and not be offended.
> 2. The scenes in the drama are not in chronological order.
> The bride is seeing the scenes as a series of flashbacks so

you will read about a sexual encounter before the couple is married.

3. Sexual references are explained through illusive imagery and symbolism. The word garden refers to the special place the husband enters. Mandrakes and pomegranates speak of fertility. Honey and wine convey intense, erotic desire.

What do you learn about God's view of sexual intimacy in the Song?

1. Write a letter to a young woman about to marry, detailing God's perspective in the Song.

Week 7

What Is It Like to Make Love with Me? Part 2

Day 1: Open the Gift of God's Blessing

Memorize Proverbs 5:18–19:

> *Let your fountain be blessed,*
> *And rejoice in the wife of your youth.*
> *As a loving hind and a graceful doe,*
> *Let her breasts satisfy you at all times;*
> *Be exhilarated always with her love.*

1. Would you feel strange if you had a picture of Jesus over your bed? Why do you think you would feel this way?

2. Read Song of Solomon 4:16—5:1. Describe God's blessing in 5:1 in your own words.

3. Have you received God's blessing on your sexual intimacy? If not, how could you do this?

4. What did you learn from Megan's story (page 129)?

5. Write a paragraph describing what it looks like for you to be able to say:

- I am forgiven!
- I am free!
- I can delight in God's gift of sex!
- I can leave Jesus' picture over the bed!

Day 2: Offer the Gift of Your Body

1. Read out loud the three versions of 1 Corinthians 7:4 on page 131. Choose one of the versions, write it here, and memorize the verse.

2. What were your feelings when you read about Kathy wrapping herself in a bow (page 132)?

3. Have you given the gift of your body to your husband? If not, how might you do this?

4. Sadie moved beyond tolerable intimacy. Do you believe God can redeem the horror of sexual abuse in you or in your friend? Explain your answer.

5. Where would you be if you believed God, if you prayed to and begged God like Sadie did? Write a prayer asking God for more in your sexual intimacy with your husband.

Day 3: What Does Everyday Lovemaking Look Like?

1. Write a paragraph describing how you felt when you read the quotes on page 132 about the fun, closeness, and planning for sexual intimacy these wives enjoyed with their husbands?

2. Describe a time you "did sex right" and how it impacted your intimate relationship with your husband.

3. Describe a time you "did sex wrong" and how it impacted your intimacy.

4. Write your own Dangerous Prayer to God about your intimacy with your husband.

Day 4: Pondering God's Word

Read through the Song of Solomon again. Ask the Holy Spirit, your Teacher, to reveal what it was like for Solomon to make love with his bride. Make a list of all you discover about her attitude, her creativity, how and when she communicated. (You will discuss this and make a combined list of what all the women found at the Bible study.)

Day 5: Pondering God's Word

Find a quiet time to be alone. Reflect on what you have learned from the Song of Solomon. Remember what you learned in the Dangerous Question "What Is It Like to Make Love with Me?" Write your declaration to God of who you desire to become as a lover to your husband.

Week 8

Why Do I Want to Stay Mad at You?

Day 1: It Feels Good to Hold a Grudge

Memorize Ephesians 4:31–32 and write it here. Also, write it on two 3 x 5 cards, and put one:

- In your purse (to pull out and meditate on at a doctor's office or waiting for your car at the repair shop).
- On the mirror where you put on your makeup each morning so you can get beautiful on the inside as you get beautiful on the outside!

1. On pages 144–145, five women expressed why it feels good to hold a grudge. Which woman do you relate to, and why?

2. What did you learn in your childhood home about forgiving? Spend time alone with God, seeking His wisdom about this for you, and then journal your thoughts.

3. Describe a time you overreacted to your husband over an insignificant incident (like a bar of soap).

4. List three to five things God revealed to you through Dana's forgiveness story on page 147.

Day 2: Three Shocking Truths about Forgiveness

1. Read 2 Corinthians 2:11. Write it here, then pray it back to God.

2. Has Satan outsmarted you? Explain how.

3. List several things you can do to kick Satan out.

4. Read the Lord's Prayer (Matt. 6:9–15) out loud. What does it look like for you to forgive your husband?

5. Is there anything you need to change about how you forgive?

6. Write a paragraph to a friend about the connection between forgiveness and intimacy with the Lord.

7. Read Proverbs 19:11 and write it here. What would give you honor and glory?

8. Make a list of the many things you learned from Katie's story on pages 152–155.

Day 3: Strip Off Anger, Put On Forgiveness

1. Go over your memory verses—Ephesians 4:31–32. List the six pieces of clothing in Ephesians 4:31 that you are to strip off, and give a definition of each one.

2. Which one is the hardest for you to "strip off"?

3. List your three new pieces of clothing in Ephesians 4:32, and give a definition of each one.

4. Which one is your "strong suit"?

5. Which one is hardest for you to "put on"? Why do you think this is difficult for you?

6. Write a short letter to a friend, expressing what you learned from Colette's story on pages 157–159.

Day 4: Anoint with Forgiveness

1. Describe the joy you feel over Connie's forgiveness anointing (pages 160–162). What delights you the most?

2. Describe your feelings about Sheryl's forgiveness anointing on pages 161–162. What grieves you the most?

3. Meditate on your memory verses, Ephesians 4:31–32. How will you be certain that you will never be saying, *If only I could have done this sooner… ?*

4. Read over quotes on pages 159–160 regarding the best things various women did for their marriages. Which one spoke to you and why?

Day 5: Be a Proactive Forgiver

1. Write a paragraph to a teenage girl sharing what a proactive forgiver is and why she should be one.

2. Write a prayer, telling God that you want to become a proactive forgiver.

3. Chose two of the practical physical symbols of forgiveness listed on pages 163–164, and explain how you will apply them in your relationship with your husband.

4. Ask yourself: What does it look like for me to be kind, tenderhearted, and forgiving toward my husband, just as God in Christ has forgiven me?

Spend some time (ten minutes or more) alone with God talking to Him about this Dangerous Question, *Why do I want to stay mad at you?*

5. Is there anything you need to ask your husband forgiveness for? How will you do this?

Week 9

Is it Possible to Grow Together When Things Fall Apart?

Day 1: An Anniversary on the Danube

1. Write James 1:2 from the three translations on page 170. Choose one of the versions to memorize.

2. Read John 16:33, Psalm 141:8, Psalm 112:7, and Isaiah 26:3. Write your view of God's perspective of trials from these verses.

3. Copy my paraphrase of James 1:2–4 for my marriage on page 170. What would you add to this paraphrase?

Day 2: Trusting God When Life Hurts

1. Read Proverbs 3:5–6 several times out loud. Write it down.

2. Describe what "trust in the Lord with all your heart" means to you personally.

3. Write a paragraph about how you live out "lean not on your own understanding."

4. What does it look like practically for you to "acknowledge God in all your ways"?

5. Write a prayer expressing your gratitude to God for His promise to make your paths straight.

Day 3: Marriage Crisis!

1. What three things did you learn from Tabi's story on page 175?

2. How was Corina creative in a hard situation (page 177)?

3. What did you feel when you read what James wrote on pages 179 about why he loves Corina?

4. Read 1 Peter 5:7 out loud. Write this verse as a prayer, thanking God that your marriage is His personal concern.

Day 4: A Long, Difficult Marriage

1. What did you learn from Natalie's story on page 180?

2. Which of Natalie's "I wills" from her Marriage Purpose Statement do you want to write out and remember?

3. What does Natalie's encouragement to a woman in a hard marriage mean to you (pages 181–183)?

4. Write Jeremiah 17:7–8 here.

5. How were these verses a reality in Natalie's life?

6. How can they be true in your life?

7. Write a note to a friend, sharing how hiding Jeremiah 17:7–8 in her heart can encourage her during time of trial.

Day 5: The Integrity Walk

1. Write out all the "I wills" you find in Psalm 101. Why do you think this psalm might have been David's Life Purpose Statement?

2. Write a paragraph sharing how Job's statement about integrity (Job 2:9–10) can impact you in times of trial in your marriage.

3. How would praying the Scriptures from this chapter help you during a trial? Write a prayer to God, based on what you read in James 1:2–4, Proverbs 3:5–6, 1 Peter 5:7, Jeremiah 17:7–8, and Job 2:10.

4. How can the four practical helps at the end of the insight (put on a "Gripes Be Gone" bracelet, write in a Thankful Journal, read the reasons you are thankful you're married to your husband, and so on) on page 188 encourage you during times of trial?

Week 10

The Woman in the Mirror

Day 1: Look at You ... a Wife by Design!
Bring your Marriage Purpose Statement to the Bible Study to share.

Read 1 Corinthians 4:2. Then memorize it.

1. What does it look like for you to look in the mirror and say, "Yes, I've been faithful. I have fulfilled my assignment as a wife to _____"?

2. Read Psalm 119:30–32. Write it here.

3. Write a paraphrase of these verses, applying them to your marriage.

4. God says as you run the faithful road, He will enlarge your heart. List three ways you need God to expand your heart toward your husband.

5. Read 1 Corinthians 4:2, write it here, and memorize it.

Day 2: God Is the Re-Creator!

1. Read pages 195–196, which talk about God being the Re-Creator. Write Proverbs 24:3–4 here.

2. What are the "precious and pleasant riches" that fill the rooms of your marriage?

3. Do you need God to re-create your marriage? Write a prayer with your specific requests for God, the Master Marriage Builder.

Day 3: The Changing Seasons of Your Marriage

1. Where are you on your marriage journey?

2. In this insight, three couples shared about their marriage journeys. Which couple did you connect with, and why did you connect with this particular one?

3. Write 1 Corinthians 13:7 here. Explain how this verse applies to you as a wife.

Day 4: Look at You: Learning! Growing! Changing!

1. What were your thoughts as you read Renee's story and Marriage Purpose Statement?

2. Read Psalm 39:4–5. Write the verses here.

3. If you really believed these verses, what difference would it make in how you loved your husband today?

Read your Marriage Purpose Statement out loud to God. Spend fifteen to thirty minutes praying about your Marriage Purpose Statement. Ask God if there is anything He wants to add to your Statement.

4. Now that you have spent these weeks reflecting on Dangerous Questions, is there anything you want to add to your Statement?

Get your calendar or PDA and write yourself a "to do" on your anniversary. On this special day, take time to reflect on your Marriage Purpose Statement. Make this your yearly anniversary habit.

Day 5: Questions to Ponder

Who asks you the hard questions? Questions like:

> Are you living your Marriage Purpose Statement?
>
> Are you walking toward your husband in love, devotion, and faithfulness?
>
> Are you being tempted to enter into an emotional or sexual affair?
>
> Are you growing in deeper intimacy with the Lord?
>
> Are you growing in deeper intimacy with your husband?

Who asks you the hard questions? A mentor? A friend? A Bible study leader or an accountability partner? If no one does, talk to God about this. Ask Him and your leader how you go about choosing someone who will.

Optional Lesson for a Twelve-Week Study

A Time of Thanksgiving, Reflection, and Celebration

For the past several weeks you've been reflecting on the question *What is it like to be married to me?* and other Dangerous Questions. You have searched God's Word and reflected on who you want to become. You are now at the end of this study, it is time to praise and thank God. This week will be a time of thanksgiving, reflection, and celebration.

THANKSGIVING (TO BE DONE ON YOUR OWN, PRIOR TO THE MEETING)
Reflect on Psalm 92:1–2, the verses you memorized the week you reflected on the Dangerous Question *Am I willing to change my attitude?* In the morning, you thanked and praised God for His lovingkindness and in the evening for His faithfulness. Make this your habit again this week.

REFLECTION (FOR YOUR STUDY DURING THE FIVE DAYS OF THE WEEK)
Day 1: Look through the chapter on the Dangerous Question *What is it like to make love with me?* Read through the Bible study, thanking God that you have new understanding about how your sexual mind-set was formed. Rejoice that you are learning new and exciting things about God's perspective about sexual intimacy—and that you are getting creative and setting the stage for intimacy with your husband.

    Day 2: Continue to reflect on *What is it like to make love with me?* Page through the chapter and read over the Bible study. Thank God that you are growing in all it means to receive His blessing on your intimacy. You've laughed about wrapping yourself in a bow but been serious about the deep meaning of giving your body as a gift to your husband. Ask God to show you one way you have grown as a lover to your husband.

    Day 3: The next Dangerous Question was about one of the most important parts of marriage, *forgiveness.* Read through "Why Do I Want to Stay Mad at You?" again, and remember why it is so important to freely forgive. You are learning how to strip off the negative and put on the positive. Forgiveness is not always easy to give or to receive, but marriage is the union of two good forgivers. Ask God to reveal one way you've grown as a "forgiver."

Day 4 is about facing trials together and asks the Dangerous Question *Is it possible to grow together when things fall apart?* Reflect on the stories of couples who have grown closer in crisis. Meditate on the many Scriptures in the Bible study that will encourage you during difficult times. Reflect on what it means to walk the Integrity Walk. Ask God to continue to reveal how you and your mate can grow closer in crisis. Write one way you can see you have grown closer to your husband during a trial.

Day 5: God is a God of hope, and He says there is hope for you and your husband. Remember that God is the Re-Creator. He loves to bring beauty out of ashes. Reflect on what you will regret and what you will not regret as a wife. Thank God that you are becoming a wife by design!

CELEBRATION (TO BE DONE PRIOR TO AND DURING YOUR GROUP TIME)
As you look back and thank God and reflect on what He has been teaching you, think of something to prepare to share with the group during your celebration time.

Your time of celebration will be during your final Bible study. Decide in advance as a group how this time will look. You could have a brunch or luncheon or meet outside if the weather is nice. Allow time for each woman to share how this study has impacted her view of God and of her role as a wife. Here are six suggestions for what you could do to prepare:

    1. Read something you wrote for an assignment.

    2. Write a letter to your daughter (daughter-in-law, grand-
       daughter, niece, special friend) expressing what you have
       learned as you've reflected on the last four Dangerous
       Questions.

3. Make an acrostic using a word like faithful, forgiving, or forever.

4. Recite memory verses that have been meaningful to you.

5. Draw a graph that shows how you have grown.

6. Write a poem or a song or paint a picture that reveals what God has taught you.

End with a time of worship and prayer, celebrating what God has done. God is faithful, and you are on the road headed toward the wife you long to become!

Notes

BY DESIGN, NOT DEFAULT

1   Attributed to the Atlanta Humane Society.

2   Author unknown.

3   Dr. Bill Bright's 1964 message.

WHAT IS REALLY IMPORTANT TO ME?

1   Thornton Wilder, *Our Town: A Play in Three Acts* (New York: HarperCollins, 2003), 100.

2   Ibid., 108.

3   Ibid., 109.

4   Ibid., 108.

5   Stephen R. Covey, *The Seven Habits of Highly Effective People* (New York: Simon and Schuster, 1989), 96.

6   Lawrence J. Crabb, Jr., and Dan Allender, *Encouragement: The Key to Caring* (Grand Rapids, MI: Zondervan, 1984), 52.

7   Used with permission.

WHAT DOES IT FEEL LIKE TO BE MY HUSBAND?

1   Author unknown.

2   Dr. Laura Schlessinger, *The Proper Care and Feeding of Husbands* (New York: Harper-Collins, 2004), 40.

3   Author unknown.

4   Schlessinger, 51.

5   Barbara Johnson, *I'm So Glad You Told Me What I Didn't Wanna Hear* (Dallas, TX: Word, 1996), 163.

6 Joyce Meyer, *The Battlefield of the Mind* (New York: Warner Faith, 1995), 69.

7 Earl D. Radmacher, *You and Your Thoughts* (Wheaton, IL: Tyndale House, 1977), 15.

8 Nancy Cobb and Connie Grigsby, *The Best Thing I Ever Did for My Marriage* (Sisters, OR: Multnomah, 2003), 83-85.

9 Charles Haddon Spurgeon, "Psalm 142:2," *The Treasury of David,* ed. Roy H. Clarke (Nashville, TN: Thomas Nelson, 1997), 654.

10 Stormie Omartian, *The Power of a Praying Wife* (Eugene, OR: Harvest House, 1997), 25–26.

11 Adapted from Will Bowen, *A Complaint Free World* (New York: Doubleday, 2007).

12 Will Bowen, *A Complaint Free World* (New York: Doubleday, 2007).

AM I WILLING TO CHANGE MY ATTITUDE?

1 Adapted from Schlessinger, *The Proper Care and Feeding of Husbands,* 12–13.

2 Nancy Leigh DeMoss, *Choosing Gratitude* (Chicago, IL: Moody Press, 2009), 50.

3 Leslie Brandt, *Psalms Now* (St. Louis, MO: Concordia, 2004).

4 Daniel Block, *The New American Commentary: Vol. 6, Judges—Ruth* (Nashville: Broadman & Holman, 1999), 605–6.

5 Beth Moore, *Living Beyond Yourself* (Nashville, TN: Lifeway Press, 1998), 157.

6 Ibid.

7 Ruth Myers, *Thirty-One Days of Praise* (Sisters, OR: Multnomah, 1994), 27.

8 Merlin Carothers, *Prison to Praise* (Escondido, CA: Merlin R. Carothers, 1970), 85.

WHAT WILL IT TAKE FOR ME TO GET CLOSE TO YOU?

1 David Minkoff, *Oy Vey: More!* (New York: St. Martin's Press, 2008), 6.

2 C. S. Lewis, *A Grief Observed* (New York: HarperCollins, 2001), 7, 47.

3 Dr. Emerson Eggerichs, *Love and Respect* (Nashville, TN: Thomas Nelson, 2004), back cover.

4 More modern words describing your important role might be *creative counterpart, completer, competent complement.*

5 *Merriam-Webster's Collegiate Dictionary,* 11th ed., s.v. "Helper."

6 Paul Lee Tan, *Encyclopedia of 7700 Illustrations* (Rockville, MD: Assurance Publishers, 1979), 71.

7 Eggerichs, *Love and Respect,* 185.

8 Ibid., 186.

WHAT IS IT LIKE TO MAKE LOVE WITH ME?

1 Eric Fuchs, *Sexual Desire and Love* (New York: Seabury Press, 1983), 108.

2 Quoted in Tim Stafford, *Sexual Chaos* (Downers Grove, IL: InterVarsity, 1993), 37.

3 Ruth Smythers, "Instruction and Advice for the Young Bride," *The Madison Institute Newsletter* (New York: Spiritual Guidance Press, Fall 1894).

4 *The Ryrie NASB Study Bible* (Chicago, IL: Moody, 2008).

WHY DO I WANT TO STAY MAD AT YOU?

1   Tan, *Encyclopedia of 7700 Illustrations,* 284.

2   Philip Yancey, *What's So Amazing About Grace?* (Grand Rapids, MI: Zondervan, 2002), 84.

3   Gabriel Garcia Marquez, *Love in the Time of Cholera* (New York: Penguin, 1989), 29–30.

4   R. T. Kendall, *Total Forgiveness* (Lake Mary, FL: Charisma House, 2007), 84.

5   Dr. Bruce K. Waltke, *The Book of Proverbs: Chapters 15—31* (Grand Rapids, MI: Eerdmans, 2005), 105.

6   Lawrence O. Richards, *Expository Dictionary of Bible Words* (Grand Rapids, MI: Zondervan, 1985), 289.

7   Dr. Joseph Dillow, Linda Dillow, Dr. Peter Pintus, and Lorraine Pintus, *Intimacy Ignited* (Colorado Springs, CO: NavPress, 2004), 215–216.

8   Allen T. Edmunds, *Reader's Digest,* January 1982, 90.

9   Tan, *Encyclopedia of 7700 Illustrations,* 456.

10 Stormie Omartian, *The Power of a Praying Wife,* 29.

IS IT POSSIBLE TO GROW TOGETHER WHEN THINGS FALL APART?

1   *Merriam-Webster's Collegiate Dictionary,* eleventh ed., s.v. "Crisis."

2   Charles R. Swindoll, *Living Beyond the Daily Grind: Book 1* (Dallas, TX: Word Publishing, 1988), 181.

3   Adapted from a prayer by Swindoll, *Living Beyond the Daily Grind: Book I,* 181.

4   Doug Weiss, one of the leading experts on sexual addiction, believes that 50 percent of Christian men are involved in pornography.

5   I cowrote this book with Jody and our good friends Lorraine and Peter Pintus. It takes you on a verse-by-verse exploration of the Song of Solomon, the Bible's manual on sex and intimacy.

6   *The Oxford English-Reader's Dictionary,* s.v. "Integrity."

7   Swindoll, *Living Beyond the Daily Grind: Book II,* 289.

THE WOMAN IN THE MIRROR

1   R. Laid Harris, Gleason L. Archer Jr., Bruce Waltke, *Theological Wordbook of the Old Testament* (Chicago: Moody Press, 1980), s.v. "bahar."

2   The Hebrew word translated "run" is *ruts,* and it means "to hasten." While the word is simply the common word for "run," interestingly, it is sometimes used of soldiers charging into battle (e.g., Joshua 8:19).

3   Ludwig Koehler, Walter Baumgardner, M.E.J. Richardson, and Johann Jakob Stamm, *The Hebrew and Aramaic Lexicon of the Old Testament* (Leiden, New York: E.J. Brill, 1999), 209.

4   Ray Boltz, *Thank You* (Nashville, TN: Thomas Nelson, 1998), 43.

5   Ibid.

6   Adapted from Swindoll, *Living Beyond the Daily Grind: Book I,* 240–41.

7   Swindoll, *Living Beyond the Daily Grind: Book I,* 241.

8   Ibid., 241.

9   Author unknown.

10 Used with permission.

11 Stephen and Judith Schwambach, *For Lovers Only* (Eugene, OR: Harvest House, 1991), 19–20.

TEN- (OR TWELVE-) WEEK REFLECTIVE BIBLE STUDY

1   Linda Dillow and Lorraine Pintus, *Intimate Issues* (Colorado Springs, CO: WaterBrook Press, 1999), 25.

2   Dr. Joseph Dillow, Linda Dillow, Dr. Peter Pintus, and Lorraine Pintus, *Intimacy Ignited* (Colorado Springs, CO: NavPress, 2004), 15.

3   Adapted from Dillow and Lorraine Pintus, *Intimacy Ignited,* 14–15.